HOW TO WRITE AND SELL FILLERS, LIGHT VERSE AND SHORT HUMOR

How to Write and Sell Fillers, Light Verse and Short Humor

Edited by
A. S. BURACK

Publishers   THE WRITER, INC.   *Boston*

Library of Congress Cataloging in Publication Data

Main entry under title:
How to write and sell fillers, light verse, and
short humor.

1. Authorship—Handbooks, manuals, etc.
I. Burack, Abraham Saul, 1908–
PN147.H667   808'.02   77-1170
ISBN 0-87116-103-6

Preface

Writing and selling short items is an excellent starting place for the beginning writer, and can lead to a profitable writing career. Fillers, short prose humor, light verse, quips, bottom-of-the-page fill-ins, recipes, jokes, epigrams, contest entries, anecdotes and unusual facts are needed by many publications, and these brief but important items can always find a place in the changing market.

This book includes twelve chapters by experienced editors and by authors who have been successful in selling their writing in the area of short verse and prose, and who share here some "how-tos" and "where-tos" to help the beginner. Most of the chapters in this book are new, although a few important chapters have been reprinted from an earlier book on the subject, and the entire volume has been updated and revised to reflect the new types of short material in demand.

Also included is a chapter on the basic rules for preparing and submitting manuscripts, plus a comprehensive market list with the names and addresses, editorial requirements and rates of pay of publications looking for short items. And in addition, you will quickly discover where and how to look for additional markets, new contests, and prize offers for recipes, slogans, or other fillers.

How to Write and Sell Fillers, Light Verse and Short Humor combines entertaining reading with sound instruction, and offers examples that are often as amusing as they are helpful.

A. S. Burack

Boston, Massachusetts

Contents

PART I

PART II

Part I

1

WRITING FILLERS AND SHORT ITEMS

by A. S. BURACK

Editor, THE WRITER *Magazine*

The fillers and short items that liven up the pages of hundreds of magazines today are becoming increasingly important to editors. Originally inserted to fill end-of-the-column and bottom-of-the-page spaces, they are now featured parts of most magazines. Many readers search out these informative and entertaining items first—skimming through the whole issue from cover to cover to find them —before they start reading the longer stories or articles.

Opportunities for writers in this field are most attractive, especially for beginners. You don't need a famous name to sell a joke, a two-line filler, a recipe or an anecdote. If you can supply editors with the kinds of fillers and short humor they want, they will buy from you even if you've never before written a single word for publication.

The time you devote to this field of writing may range from a full daily schedule to a part-time hobby—or just an occasional try at breaking into print with a quip, verse, or other brief item. It's the kind of writing that can be done at any time and in almost any place. You can keep regular working hours at your desk, or you can fit your planning and writing in among your usual everyday activities. A considerable amount of writing can be done while you are commuting to work, doing household chores, eating lunch, or even when you are convalescing from an illness. There is hardly a time during the day when you cannot collect ideas for publishable short items. Listen to the quips or amusing anecdotes related by your co-workers. Train yourself to "hear" the bright sayings of children. Watch for the unusual or helpful solution to a problem. Make mental notes of these—and then get them down on paper at the first opportunity.

Your reading, too, can be productive. Look for clever phrases, humorous errors in print, interesting or little-known facts—all these can bring you dividends. And remember, also, that although new and original ideas are always needed and wanted by editors, no subject, no matter how commonplace, should be ignored as possible filler material. For example, how to train a new puppy—or how you trained your family to take care of a new puppy—may find a place in some magazine (you might try some humor for this subject). Each December, magazines want to remind Christmas tree owners of certain fire prevention rules; a brief list of these, properly written up, is bound to find a market. Each spring, some magazine will tell its readers how to recognize and treat poison ivy; next year, it could be *your* little article on this subject that will appear in print.

There are innumerable markets for short items of every variety, and the payment ranges from pin money to substantial sums. *American Legion Magazine* pays $10 for one-line epigrams and $20 for original anecdotes. A handy man or woman can get from $5 to $75 for shop or home short-cuts and fillers from *Mechanix Illustrated.* Rates for short filler material at *Catholic Digest* range from $4 to $50. *The New Yorker* pays $5 and up for amusing typographical errors and anecdotes. Homemakers may receive $25 for brief practical suggestions and short items on instructive family experiences from *Woman's Day. Playboy* pays $50 for jokes and $50 to $350 for brief, amusing paragraphs on topical subjects. *The Reader's Digest* pays $35 to $300 for a wide variety of material, including items for "Toward More Picturesque Speech," "Campus Comedy," "Life in These United States," "Laughter, the Best Medicine," "Personal Glimpses," "Humor in Uniform," "All in a Day's Work," "Points to Ponder," "Quotable Quotes," and "Notes from All Over."

Practically everything you do is a possible source of ideas for short items. Cleaning a closet may give you ideas for a humorous paragraph or two—or perhaps you'll be able to write up an efficient way of dealing with this chore. If you've given or attended a successful party recently, remember that novel party ideas are always in demand—special decorations for children's parties, menus and games for teen-agers, shower ideas, etc. Do you have any organic gardening tips? Many magazines are interested in them. Have you made a lamp from some unusual materials? Helpful decorating features will almost always find a market. Hints on child-rearing can bring many small checks. How do you handle the problem of traveling with children? This could be the subject of a helpful article or it could be written up humorously. Have you worked out a clever merchandising scheme for your business? Do you have a short cut that has proved helpful in your job? There are trade and business publications for almost every business or profession, and these may welcome write-ups of such ideas.

Writing short items requires no special training. Editors are primarily interested in helpful information they can pass on to their readers. Ideas should be set down clearly and simply. Keep in mind that the style used in most fillers—from short fact articles to one-line hints—is informal, conversational.

When you write up an article for publication, pretend that you are sharing an idea, a hint or a story with someone you know. The friendly approach brings good results.

Here are a few basic points to keep in mind when writing an idea:

1) First and foremost, ask yourself, "Do I have a solution to a problem?" The "problem" may be something as simple as what to feed hungry children when they come home from school, but your item should offer a real solution to a common problem. And, speaking of common problems, your next question should be, "Do people who read this publication have this problem, so that the editor will feel it belongs in his pages?"

2) Next, consider the appeal of your idea. Will it be interesting and helpful to readers? If you want to submit some recipes, ask yourself if they are easy to prepare, nutritious and economical. Would the dishes have eye-appeal; do they tempt fussy appetites? Also, have you checked your recipe carefully? Be sure ingredients and

timing are correct when you submit recipes—your dishes must turn out right in the magazines' test kitchens.

3) How-to-do-it pieces must also be precise and detailed. Have you made your directions simple enough for any amateur to follow? Are all of the measurements accurate in your description of how to build a coffee table from scrap lumber? It's best to give step-by-step instructions—either number your directions or say, "First, prepare this. Then, do that," etc. Always suggest substitutes for material or equipment that may not be available in some areas. This is particularly important to magazines with national circulations.

4) One last point: timeliness. While editorial schedules and needs differ, chances are that an editor will not be buying hints for Christmas decorations in November; at that time the Christmas issue is already being printed or is on the newsstands, and few editors like to save material for a whole year. Therefore, holiday, special occasion or seasonal material should usually be submitted to monthly magazines from four to seven months in advance, and eight or ten weeks ahead to weekly publications.

You may not be able to decide immediately what form your idea should take—should it be written up as a brief hint, or should you expand it to a short feature? Should you give it a humorous or serious treatment? This will often depend upon your own experience and temperament. If something strikes you as funny, perhaps you should try the humorous approach; if it's the *information* that mainly interests you, write it up factually. Sometimes it's best to gather several related ideas and present them as a brief feature built around a central theme.

When you send accompanying diagrams or photographs,

be sure these are as clear as possible. In case your own photographs do not turn out well, it will be worth your while to arrange for a competent amateur to take the pictures. Payment arrangements for this vary, but most of the time you can pay the photographer a certain percentage of your check. Moreover, you'll find that many magazines pay extra for photographs.

In this "read-as-you-run" age, fillers, quips, anecdotes, etc. will receive careful reading in the editorial offices of hundreds of publications. Editors always need fresh sources of supply to keep their stock of material varied and up-to-date. *Your* brief contributions may find a ready welcome in their pages.

2

SHORT PROSE HUMOR THAT WILL SELL

by RICHARD ARMOUR

A leading humorist and light verse writer

Two of the hardest forms of writing to publish these days are poetry and fiction. But that doesn't disturb me the slightest, because I don't write either.

My bent—and with the passing years I am growing more bent than ever—is humor, humor which takes the form of light nonfiction rather than fiction, and light verse rather than poetry.

If you study the market lists in such an inclusive and reliable reference work as *The Writer's Handbook,* you will find "humor," "humorous pieces, 1,000 to 2,000 words," "humorous or human-interest articles," "satire, sophisticated humor," "light treatment, lively, enjoyable style," and so on.

Or study the magazines themselves, as I do. Often I find

a magazine that uses humor occasionally and yet makes no mention of it in a market list. Sometimes a magazine that is "staff written" or "takes no unsolicited manuscripts," such as *National Lampoon,* may break its rules, I have discovered. But you must come up with something unusual and really good, and it would be wise to query first and describe briefly what you have written. This is a long shot, and you may discover you are shooting blanks, but it is worth a try.

However, there are better possibilities. Markets for humor exist, in fact are numerous, but you must ferret them out. But before I say anything more about markets, I should say something about writing what is marketable. The competition is keen, and before you become obsessed with markets, you must learn how to write humor that editors cannot resist.

This is not easy. It is as hard to make readers laugh as it is to make them cry. In my book, *Writing Light Verse and Prose Humor* (The Writer, Inc.), I go into subject matter, techniques, length, openings and endings, titles, and everything you had always wanted to know but were afraid to ask (or didn't know whom to ask) about this minor but exacting form of writing.

In humor, as in any kind of writing, quantity usually comes before quality. That is, you must write much before you write well. And along with your writing do some reading. Read, study, and analyze the writings of humorists you admire. Notice the subjects they write about, how they catch the reader in the first sentence (S.J. Perelman is a master at this), and how they play with words. Notice how they use overstatement (exaggeration) or its opposite, understatement, turning something generally thought important into something trivial. Notice whether they are writing to amuse or, in the role of satirist, to debunk, deflate, point out a wrong that should be righted.

As for which writers of humor you might read and learn from, you have a wide choice. Times have changed, but all types of humor are still being written. Instead of Will Rogers, we have Art Buchwald. Instead of Robert Benchley and James Thurber, we have Tom Wolfe and Kurt Vonnegut. Along with the new-fashioned humor, tending to satire, there is still far more old-fashioned humor of the home-and-family sort than many think. It's the kind Erma Bombeck writes in her syndicated column, and Jean Kerr and Sam Levenson write in their books—some of it sophisticated and some of it not sophisticated.

Prose humor can take the form of either fiction or nonfiction. A short story can be light, even funny. Indeed it may be wild and zany, or it may be merely playful, or have touches that give comic relief to what would otherwise be totally serious. Humorous or light prose has possibilities that light verse does not. It can go beyond the short piece in a newspaper or the short story in a magazine to the novel or even to the stage—or screen. There is always the chance, however slight, that a humorous piece can be the basis of a Broadway hit or a film with a major comic star like Woody Allen. You can dream, can't you? I hope you can, because that is one of the things that keeps a writer writing.

One further advantage of writing humor in prose is that it can be almost any length, whereas light verse must be kept short (usually four to twelve lines). A good marketable length for nonfiction prose humor is around 1,500 words, but certain publications, ranging from *Parents'* to *Playboy*—I have written for both—use humor articles (obviously of very different kinds) as long as 3,000 words. A piece of prose humor can be more than a filler—it can be a feature article that will be listed in the table of contents. This gives the writer more of a showcase and may lead to bigger, if not better, things.

Though most of my prose humor runs to about 1,500 words and rarely more than 2,000, I like to do even shorter pieces: 300 to 400 words for Martin Levin's "The Phoenix Nest," formerly in the *Saturday Review* but now syndicated by the Associated Press, and fillers half that length for "Post Scripts" in *The Saturday Evening Post*.

To illustrate what can be done in small space and to give you some humor to analyze, here is a short one, about 300 words, that I sold to "The Phoenix Nest":

LISTEN TO THIS

Some people talk too much, and I happen to be one of them. Actually I know I should talk only half as much as I listen. The reason is obvious: I have two ears but only one mouth.

This proportion of ears to mouth is not peculiar to me. Everyone is the same in this regard, and there must have been some reason for making us this way. Have you ever seen anyone with two mouths and one ear? Would you like to have two mouths and one ear yourself? And if you had two mouths, and could talk out of both of them at once, where would you like them placed?

My two ears are very well situated, and I have no desire to shift their location or to have any extras. But two mouths raise some intriguing possibilities for anyone who likes to talk.

They might be side by side, and I could confuse people by simultaneously saying "No" with one and "Yes" with the other, or talking at the same time on two subjects. I might even sing a duet all by myself, which would have to be heard to be believed.

Having a second mouth in the back of my head might be

useful in shouting at pursuers. Having a mouth on top of my head would enable me to speak up, in more ways than one, to those taller than I.

But it looks as though I am going to have to get along with one mouth, and where it is. All I can say is that anyone who knows me will tell you I ought to keep it closed more. And I shouldn't forget that my Maker, in giving me one mouth and two ears, knew what He was doing. I should take the hint—and that goes for a few others I know.

That's no classic, no great work of humor, but perhaps it shows you what can be done in a few words with a small but universal subject. It opens with a simple truth, and I point the finger of ridicule at myself. It closes with a hint that I am not alone in what I make fun of. In between, in short, simple sentences, it is an exercise in imagination and ridiculousness.

The human body, which is something everyone has, is a good subject for humor. I did much longer pieces for *Playboy* on the elbow ("Looking Over the Overlooked Elbow") and on the lips, and I have done playful articles on the nose, chin, feet, and fingernails for other magazines. Yes, I even did a piece about the thumb, called "Thumbthing to Think About."

Like Erma Bombeck, I have found a rich harvest of subjects for humor in the home: the husband-wife relationship, coping with problems that arise with children and grandchildren, struggling with bugs and weeds in the garden, keeping the garage uncluttered enough to have room to park our car, and so on. Sometimes I have mixed humor and moralizing, as in "Confessions of a Faulty Father" in *Family Circle* and "Humor to the Rescue" in *Parents' Magazine.*

But I have also written sharper, more intellectual satire

for markets as varied politically as *The New York Times* and the *National Review*. The latter, by the way, is listed under "Fillers and Humor" in *The Writer's Handbook* as looking for "satire, to 900 words."

It is good to write on many subjects and in different ways, though you may discover you are better in one area than another. I confess I would like to be a political and social satirist, syndicated as widely as Art Buchwald. But with a few exceptions, such as a Swiftian piece of irony called "How to Burn a Book" that originally appeared in an educational magazine and then was reprinted many times in magazines and newspapers in this country and in England, I am resigned to the fact that I am better at writing playfully about personal yet universal trivia.

Yes, my forte is toying with subjects such as plastic plants, paper clips, losing my glasses case, wire coat hangers, or my neighbor's leaves that suddenly become mine. This last led me to write an article called "Leaf Me Alone." By writing a playful piece about something that vexed me, instead of complaining to my neighbor (who is bigger than I am), I got a substantial check instead of a black eye. But I try to write more than one kind of humor, keeping my options open, and perhaps you will find it wise to do the same.

Despite what many say, humor is not dead. Maybe sick humor is, after getting more and more sickening, and that's all right with me. I try to write healthy humor, perhaps because I have a healthy respect for humor, and when I have written it, I try to find a market for it. Usually, but not always, I do. I have to hunt harder than I once did, but I am a determined hunter. Perhaps I need a bird dog, or a word dog.

The world needs humor today and, fortunately, some editors are aware of this. All you have to do to get your humor published is to write publishable humor, and then find the right place for it. It is as simple as that. As a matter of fact I once wrote, and published, an article on the so-called funny bone. What is funny about the funny bone is that there is nothing funny about it.

So far I have been weaving back and forth between writing and marketing. After all, writing is only half of it. Selling what you write is the other half. Or maybe my proportions are wrong. Perhaps it is one-third and two-thirds. Or one-tenth and nine-tenths. Of course, you may be the kind who writes for the sheer joy of it, for expression of self, or for therapy.

I write for all these reasons, but mostly, I admit, I write to be published, to be paid, to be read. If that is a crass, commercial, lowbrow reason for writing, so be it. It has been my chief motivation since I began to write humor for *The New Yorker* and *The Saturday Evening Post* in 1937.

Times have changed. It is not that there is less humor or poorer humor or fewer humorists, but there are fewer markets for humor today. Almost the only humor left in *The New Yorker* is in the cartoons. *The Saturday Evening Post* died, but then came back to life—or a reasonable facsimile thereof—as a kind of museum piece. It uses humor, on the "Post Scripts" pages and elsewhere, but much less because it comes out nine times a year (though moving toward twelve), instead of weekly. *Look* was one of the magazines that was once a good market for humor but has now disappeared. Other magazines have stopped using humor or are staff written.

And yet I continue to publish about 200 pieces of

humor (both articles and light verse) a year. If the markets for humor are so few, how do I manage this?

I have discovered a whole new world of markets for humor—the world of specialty magazines. An unlikely place for humor, you might think, would be a medical magazine, but I wrote a feature called "The Medical Muse" for *Postgraduate Medicine* every month for twenty-three years. Then, as often happens, a new editor came in and "The Medical Muse" went out.

But I had opened a crack, or cracked an opening, in the medical field, and I have since written humor for *The Journal of the American Medical Association, Geriatrics,* and *Family Health.* For *Family Health* I wrote on such subjects as doctors' names, the common cold (both articles reprinted in the *Reader's Digest*), arthritis, acupuncture, and I don't know what all.

I have discovered that you don't have to be an expert in a field to write human-interest humor about it. Perhaps it helps *not* to know too much. Your very ignorance may be funny. Of course, you must know a little about the subject, which is why I have become a regular reader of medical journals, and now imagine I have all the diseases I read about.

Similarly, you should at least be interested in sports before you write a humor piece for *Sports Illustrated,* or in travel in the western United States before you submit an item to *Westways.* And you should know and care about fine foods before you try a humorous piece for *Gourmet*— and so on. But you need to know far less about these specialized subjects than writers who write serious articles for such magazines.

There are many regional magazines that use humor and pay well. I live in Southern California and write a regular monthly humor article for one magazine and an occasional piece for another, both of them what you might call West Coast *New Yorkers.* No doubt your part of the country has similar magazines. If not, there is probably a newspaper in your region that might be receptive to humor with local color, even if the paper carries Art Buchwald or Russell Baker or some other syndicated columnist. My paper is the *Los Angeles Times,* and I have written several lightserious, sometimes satirical, articles for its Op-Ed page.

Or consider the specialized field of airline in-flight publications. I have written humorous articles, or factual articles with a touch of humor, for the magazines of such airlines as Western, American, TWA, and United. One was on clouds, one on man's attempts to imitate birds, one on why I like an aisle seat, and so on. Some took a bit of research; others came out of experience and imagination. All were mostly written in the spirit of fun.

The article market list in *The Writer's Handbook* under "General Magazines" is relatively short as compared with fifty pages of periodicals listed under such headings as "Religious and Denominational Magazines," "Sports, Outdoors, Recreation, and Conservation," and "Women's Magazines; Home and Garden Publications," as well as fifty more pages of what are called "Specialized Magazines," in such fields as health, education, performing arts, photography, hobbies, technical and scientific, trade and business, travel, and city and regional.

Here is a rich mother lode, or even father lode, for the writer of humor. It has never been fully explored. I have not sent a piece of humorous prose or verse to *Progressive Grocer, The Church Musician,* or *Popular Electronics,* but they tempt me. I'll wager that, whether they know it

or not, they could use some humor. Their readers would
be grateful.

With humor markets as they are today, I suggest trying
what might seem the most unlikely places, the highly specialized magazines. Maybe the editor is a little bored and
just ripe for a little something with which to lighten his
pages. And maybe your kind of humor (or mine) is what,
without knowing it, he has been waiting for.

The most important thing I learned, long ago, is to keep
a large number of pieces in the mail. I always have fifty or
more in my "Pieces Out" folder, and even more in the
hands of editors—where I hope most of them will stay.
That's the only way you can expect sales. I do have some
regular markets that buy almost everything I send them.
But, alas, there are only a few of these.

Keeping lots of items in the mail makes it worthwhile
to watch for the mailman. He is my cash register.

3

THE READER'S DIGEST
AS A FILLER MARKET

by **MARY T. DILLON**
Formerly Senior Editor, THE READER'S DIGEST

After weeks of searching San Diego for a position suitable to a young man of my abilities and education, I was forced to take a job cleaning apartments for a maintenance company. I soon found that this "woman's job" was hard work. The real feeling of role reversal came, however, one day while I was cleaning a vacant apartment. Answering a knock at the door, I was startled to see an attractive young woman in brown coveralls, wearing a utility belt filled with tools.

"Hi," she said. "I'm the telephone man, here to disconnect the phone."

"Oh?" I answered. "Come on in. I'm the cleaning lady."
—Jay Bracone *(Kennesaw, GA)*

We knew our search for the right veterinarian had ended when, upon our second visit to his office, the good doctor patted our beloved dog and said, "Sam, so good to see you." Then, with

27

just a trace of embarrassment, he looked at my husband and asked, "What's your name again, sir?"

—Clarice Parrish *(Wilburton, OK)*

We were delighted with the conscientious service provided by our newspaper carrier, who was a graduate student at the university. One day we received a note from him telling us not to worry if our paper should be late one morning during the weeks ahead. He was participating in husband-coached childbirth and would, of course, have to be with his wife when their baby was born.

My husband and I, therefore, felt relieved when the day came that our paper did not arrive on time. We wondered if the new father would send a follow-up note to tell everyone on his route the news.

Several mornings later, I heard my husband chuckling as he came in with the paper, which had been neatly tied with a bright pink bow.

—Susan M. Lefler *(Lexington, KY)*

At the bakery counter in our local supermarket, I saw an attractive woman loading her cart with packaged cupcakes. Curiosity got the better of me. "Why so many?" I asked.

"These are going-home presents," she replied.

"Going-home presents?"

"My back yard," she explained, "is mecca for the neighborhood children. When I can't stand the noise any longer, I call out to them to be sure to come to the back door when they are through playing and take a present home. In seconds, it's blissfully quiet. Works every time!"

—Mrs. Thomas Sigethy *(Naples, FL)*

Several years ago, I got a well-deserved speeding ticket which directed me to appear before a judge in Park City, Utah. But in that sleepy mining town tucked back in the hills, the trick was to find the judge. The one inhabitant in view reckoned I'd likely find the judge at home, and pointed to a frame house halfway up the canyon.

My knock was answered by a somewhat flushed, motherly-looking woman, wiping her hands on her apron. The judge, it seemed, was canning peaches. When I stated my business, she asked, "How do you plead?" "Guilty," I said meekly. "Oh, dear, too bad," murmured Her Honor sympathetically, as she rummaged through a bureau for a receipt.

Official business over, the judge, who'd spotted my English accent, put on the teakettle, and we settled down for a chat about people and places in England. As I reluctantly drove off into the sunset—two jars of golden peaches on the seat beside me—I turned for a last glimpse of the good judge, as she stood waving me on my way. Truly the most pleasant day in court I ever hope to spend!

—Jacqueline Meyer *(Salt Lake City, UT)*

The above, all of them typical anecdotes published in the famous "Life in These United States" department of *The Reader's Digest,* are the sort of everyday-life anecdotes readers have come to connect with *The Digest.* They narrate incidents that might have happened almost anywhere and yet there's something a little special about each one of them. A "Life in These United States" story may afford an insight into human nature, convey a regional flavor, prompt a kindly chuckle at an individual foible or a sympathetic grin at the plight of a human being in a familiar dilemma. "Life" stories may even teach a lesson, if the moral is pointed gently.

These stories, which ordinarily don't exceed 300 words, almost invariably say a lot in a little. Articles have been written about the American disease of automobilitis, but the point was made more succinctly by Mrs. Winifred Enright of Buffalo:

I never realized how seldom I went out without the car until I overheard an observation made by my daughter. She and a friend were approaching the back door when the other girl said, "Maybe nobody's home."

"Oh, yes, there is," my daughter replied. "The car's in—and we never leave the car home alone."

"Life in These United States," one of the popular continuing features of *The Reader's Digest,* is made up entirely of material contributed by the magazine's readers and has appeared almost every month since inauguration of the department in March 1943. Doubtless, many readers of this book have at one time or another sent in a story in the hope of earning the payment, now $300, offered for acceptable 300-word anecdotes.

Original anecdotes are also solicited for "All in a Day's Work" (humorous incidents on the job), "Campus Comedy" and "Humor in Uniform," at the same rate of $300.

"Life in These United States" currently receives more than 10,000 pieces of mail monthly. In addition, some 15,000 reader contributions are directed to other departments of the magazine each month; these include published items as well as original anecdotes and quips. Altogether the total of individual items submitted runs up to more than a quarter of a million yearly.

These formidable statistics seem enough to discourage any would-be contributor to the pages of the world's most widely read magazine. But there is no real reason for discouragement. The solicitation of material for various departments of *The Digest* is in no sense a contest in which one's chances may diminish as the number of contestants increases. It is simply a part of the continuing search for the best possible editorial material.

Experience has taught the editors that in their own

readers is a never-failing vein of editorial gold, truly the mother lode as far as excerpt material goes. As a result, *The Reader's Digest* is perhaps the most "contributed to" of any large general magazine. Few readers are aware, as they leaf through *The Digest*'s pages in search of the bright quips, amusing or heartwarming anecdotes and thought-provoking quotes that enliven each issue, that about half of the 135 or so short items in any month's *Digest* have been sent in from "outside"—a statistic that should provide real encouragement for free-lance contributors.

In evaluating items, what is it that the editors are searching for? Requirements for the various departments differ, of course. They are briefly indicated in the announcement about contributions which appears in the magazine each month. But the characteristics of a usable story are exceedingly difficult to define, and the best way to determine them is to study the material appearing in the magazine itself. An effort is made to avoid stereotypes; an occasional quip may even be selected simply because it *doesn't* sound like *The Reader's Digest*. But still *The Digest* itself is the best teacher, and the contributor should go over several copies before sending in material. He should note the various regular departments. While only previously unpublished items are acceptable for "Life in These United States," some of the other departments—"Toward More Pictureseque Speech," "All in a Day's Work," "Campus Comedy," "Humor in Uniform" and "Laughter, the Best Medicine"—may include a mixture of original and in-print items. "Personal Glimpses," "Quotable Quotes," "Points to Ponder" and "Notes From All Over" rely primarily on published material. The contributor should also study the fillers which follow articles in the magazine. There are some frequently used titles, like "Pardon, Your Slip Is

Showing," "Signs of Life," "Caught in Passing," "Headline Hits," which suggest areas in which reader contributions are welcome. In addition he should consider the individual fillers, ranging from one line to almost a page in length, and filler groups in a wide variety of categories. The Excerpt Department has some 600 different headings under which items are organized, all the way from Absent-Minded and Advice through Modern Lingo and Money Matters to Zany and Zoo Stories.

You will probably direct your contribution to a specific department, and indeed you are asked to do so. But don't fear that your contribution will be overlooked if it doesn't fit the needs of the department to which it was addressed. Outstanding items are passed from editor to editor, and all concerned make an effort to find the proper niche for an anecdote or quip or quote that has genuine appeal.

Payment is made on the basis of the item's final disposition. Thus a story submitted to "Life in These United States" but used in "Laughter, the Best Medicine," or as a filler, would not pay its contributor $300. The payment for original material used in "Laughter, the Best Medicine," "Personal Glimpses," and elsewhere is $15 per *Digest* two-column line. It is not *Digest* policy to acknowledge or return short contributions, but an exception will be made when a self-addressed stamped envelope is enclosed.

Quite a large proportion of *Digest* excerpts are reprinted from other published sources. These items are found in a variety of ways. Staff members covering syndicated columns and other good sources locate many of the items that are used. Also, certain outside contributors have been immensely helpful in this area, some of them working hard at the job of contributing reprint items to *The Digest*.

Likely sources for outside contributors are local newspapers (watch for clever headlines, funny ads, amusing typographical errors), non-syndicated columns, regional publications. Excellent items have even been found in annual reports, in the folders that sometimes accompany telephone bills, in advertisements and pamphlets. Television talk shows may yield usable material. Some of the best fillers have been stories told at a party or fragments of overheard conversation.

Less likely as excerpt source material are the national magazines, which are carefully covered by *The Digest*. Joke books are not a very good source to draw on—the staff has probably beaten the non-staffer to any such obvious possibility. Other books, though, may yield "Quotable Quotes," items for "Picturesque Speech," "Personal Glimpses," "Points to Ponder," etc.

In submitting previously published material, remember to give full sources including page references, with place of publication as well as names of newspapers. It is helpful to have submissions pasted or typed singly on separate sheets, with the name and address of the contributor and the date of the contribution on each sheet. This facilitates the above-described passing about of items for consideration for different departments of the magazine. Payment of $35 is made to the first contributor of an item from a published source.

But what *is* it that sells a story to *The Digest*? One member of the staff tells me he has one general rule: He never passes over anything that makes him either laugh out loud or feel a lump in his throat. These are subjective reactions, it's true, but remember that they are reactions of an experienced editor. As such, they are indicative. The doctored-up "gag," the contrived story, won't usually prompt this sort of direct emotional response. If you find yourself laughing uproariously and wholeheartedly at a humorous experience or being touched by a poignant or heartwarming incident, stop and ask yourself if you haven't just been exposed to a bit of genuine "Life in These United States." If the answer is yes, get to a typewriter right away and set the story down in rough draft while its details are clear in your mind.

Frequently received (by the thousands!) but not often used are stories turning on the bright sayings or clever actions of children. There are few parents who can resist the temptation to talk about their children, and such stories often have undeniable appeal. But to be selected for publication they must be *really outstanding.* After all, there'd be little point in printing a story about a child who struck the reader as being no brighter or more charming than his own young hopeful.

The Digest editorial staff ordinarily fails to find anything very funny in practical jokes or in stories whose humor results from the fact of a person's ethnic origin or physical handicap. A large proportion of rejected stories fall into these general categories.

Also summarily discarded is the frankly pornographic story. Here again we are involved in considerations of good taste. Just as stories involving cruelty of one sort or another seem to us to offend good taste, so certain sex stories are unthinkable for *The Reader's Digest.* But the fact that a story has sex overtones does not in itself rule it out. Since sex is a part of human life, stories dealing cleverly and honestly with it are acceptable to *The Digest,* as they are today to most general magazines.

The Reader's Digest needs and wants good filler material. Readers of this book are urged to keep the magazine in mind as a market for their very best short items.

4

FILLERS, QUIPS AND EPIGRAMS

by **SELMA GLASSER**
Successful free-lance writer and columnist

My kind of writing—fillers, short items, and prize contests—employs all kinds of puns, parodies and plays on
words imaginable. I pluck popular expressions, proverbs,
and current slang out of newspapers—and out of people's
mouths—then utilize them with a twist and a turn, this
way and that way, to convert them into salable shorts.
Since I am currently selling fillers to most of the major
national magazines and winning writing contests for a
variety of short items, my mind has become conditioned
to detect usable phrases and give them a fresh or unusual
curve, bend or blend. Besides, ideas can be, and usually are,
found everywhere if only we look for them—on billboards,
in shop windows—and timely, topical subjects are also a
good source.

Let me give you an example of a current phrase that I thought I might arrange differently with a change of a consonant or two. The words *women's liberation, libbers, lib* pop up in print and in conversations all the time. Somehow these suggest another much-used but ordinary phrase which is not humorous in itself but somehow evokes smiles when said. I blended the two together and arrived at this play on words, which ultimately appeared in *Playboy*.

Timid feminist—*chicken libber*

That was an easy one, converting a current topic or popular expression into a similar-sounding pun or parody. It is clear at a glance, recognizable and possesses a certain amount of humor.

Thus encouraged, I've been creating every short cut on the road to writing imaginable! If I can earn up to $50 and more for a brief filler, why should I write at length? That is what *Playboy* paid me for the word "transplant" interpreted in this manner.

A medium's place for holding seances is called: *the trance plant.*

Playing with words, phrases and clichés is probably what I do most in my short writing. Sometimes I delve into discovering literal meanings of commonly used, popular words and phrases. I pull them apart and show how different their current usage is as compared to their actual meanings. It provides a unique type of filler for me. Here are a few ordinary words—*Ticker Tape, Old-Timer, the Cold War*—that I recently sold to "Light Housekeeping" (*Good Housekeeping*):

TWO-WAY BRAIN TEASERS

What's an electrocardiograph?	*ticker tape*
What would you call an ancient watch?	*old-timer*
What do antibiotics fight?	*the cold war*

Sometimes a word and/or phrase will trigger a filler idea. For instance, when *The Grapes of Wrath* was being discussed within my hearing, it suggested two different salable fillers to me. The first version sold to *Wall Street Journal* as:

Demonstrations: *groups of wrath*

The second appeared in *The American Journal of Nursing,* and went like this:

Holiday hangover: *the wrath of grapes*

Everybody talks about car pools these days. The first time I heard that expression, a humorous interpretation of the phrase hit me. I developed it into a question-and-answer piece for *Good Housekeeping* which went like this:

Where should folks take their automobile swimming?
In car pools.

Good Housekeeping bought it for their "Light Housekeeping" page for about $100. I added a few more, such as:

Question: What do you do if you give up spinach?
Answer: Scrap iron.
Question: What's an Indian?
Answer: Early American.

How many times have we heard the expression, "little things count"? Here is an example of how I converted an everyday phrase into a double-entendre epigram and sold it to *Family Weekly* for their "Quips and Quotes" column.

A kindergarten teacher is a woman who knows how to make little things count.

Another case comes to mind. All of us have been the targets of uncalled-for remarks and resented them. The last straw broke this camel's back—and when I'm angry I write. While I was fuming, this epigram practically wrote itself, and was sold to *Family Weekly*:

Remarks that are uncalled for are usually delivered.

It was reprinted shortly thereafter in *The Reader's Digest*, and this tended to assuage my anger further.

Current, timely subjects are always available to us. Air pollution, for example, is discussed constantly. It's like the weather, which everyone talks about, but no one does anything about. Well, the best I could do was to write a "daffynition" which sold to *The Wall Street Journal*:

Air pollution: *fume fatale*

Sometimes a straight sign that you see day after day can be worked into a filler. For example, what would you do with these two? "Avoid Home Accidents" and "Watch Out For Children."

Here's how I sold it to *Medical World News*:

Signs of the Times: Planned parenthood isn't anything new. For years we've observed signs and seen warnings like: "Avoid Home Accidents" and "Watch Out for Children."

Idea starters are everywhere. A while back, I found myself in a greeting card store. I noticed a Hallmark card which featured several simple puns. When I returned home, I started to compile my own original but ridiculous puns. Shortly thereafter, Hallmark bought them, and I can honestly say, I got a high price for some very low puns.

You might well ask where I find such well-paying markets. Instead of participating in such active sports as golf, tennis or handball, I plop myself down in an easy chair and thoroughly review contest and writers' magazines I write articles and columns for, plus any random magazines members of the family buy. Once in a while, I spend time sitting around at the library perusing all the current issues of the better magazines to see what fillers they're buying and what prices they're paying. When I'm waiting my turn to check out at the supermarket, I don't waste a minute. I spend the time scanning all the weekly publications for sale, looking for their write-in fillers. Newsstands and bookstores intrigue me as well, and I find myself browsing endlessly, searching for useful information to further my writing career. A daily newspaper, carefully scanned, can sometimes open up new writing horizons. One such item, properly utilized, led me to writing gags for Joan Rivers.

Everything can present a new opportunity for you. When I wait at the doctor's or dentist's, I usually unearth countless new markets and magazines. Unfortunately (or should I say fortunately), I'm in good health and have fairly good teeth. Therefore, I don't get to see these medical men often, but any visit pays for itself many times over. Unquestionably, the way I manage to keep abreast of what's doing in the filler field is the number one secret to my writing success. My desire to compete is number two. Thirdly, I really love to write, especially if I don't have to be too wordy about it.

There's no substitute for writing constantly and keeping what you write—fillers, slogans, contest entries, limericks, and other short items—in the mail.

5

HOW TO BE EXCRUCIATINGLY FUNNY IN SHORTS

by ROBERT FONTAINE
Humorist, novelist, and playwright

The editor of this tutti-frutti collection has approached me
sideways and offered me a controlling interest in the
Panama Canal if I will reveal my methods of writing humorous shorts. I have agreed to the offer, but I must explain to
the reader that I am not really completely aware of how I
do it myself. On the other hand, I have always had one eye
on the Panama Canal.

Let me say, by way of preface, that there is not much
difference between writing funny short pieces and funny
long pieces. The short pieces are usually not quite as long.
A short funny piece may be made into a longer one by in-
serting a few more typewritten pages under the paper clip.

Furthermore, not everybody laughs at funny pieces.

Most editors, for example, never laugh at funny pieces. They have seen so many of mine that if they were to let themselves go they would be just plain worn out. What an editor does when he reads something funny is sort of twitch on one side, scrape his throat, wrinkle up his nose and give an abortive sneeze. It gives the general impression he is suffering from a rare tropical tic picked up while trying to talk an Andaman Islander Shaman into ghosting an article on his tribe's puberty rites.

I should make an exception here. I know one or two editors who *say* they laugh at my comical pieces. I have before me notes like this: "I and the whole staff are still rocking with laughter over the piece on meat loaves you sent us. It certainly brightened up our day and no one knows how much I regret it isn't possible to buy it. Do try us again." (That'll be the day!)

Sometimes I get a picture, from reading these notes, that a few unbridled editors are running a shop where all the staff from the charwoman up are so busted up with laughter after reading my shorts that they can barely stuff the things into return envelopes.

What I am trying to say, seriously, is that nobody knows what a funny short piece is. We all know what a short piece is, but "funny" is something else again. In my youth when I wore bangs and played the flute and was dreadfully naive, I used to try to figure out what *other* people would think was funny. This never worked either, so I reverted to the "Big I" system or "What I think is funny is funny and any editor who doesn't agree, may his newsstand sales drop twenty-two percent in Kenosha!" This also doesn't work, but it makes me feel better because if nobody in the business laughs at some of my things, you can bet that I do.

Anyone who reads a short piece of mine in some journal and thinks, "This isn't a bit funny," might like to know I laughed myself sidesaddle writing it. My wife and family also laughed at it or they didn't get any dinner that night.

In all sweet solemnity, there is one nice thing about making up short funnies. If no one ever buys them you have a lot of droll remarks to make at parties. What's more, short humor is the only thing I write that I thoroughly enjoy, and if anybody wants to give me money for it, it's like velvet blankets over silk sheets—so much the better.

Well, here I am rambling on about myself and not a word about you. You want, I suppose, to know how I go about plying my trade. First, I do a lot of thinking. I do this mostly when there is no one home because I find it trying to think when anyone is in the house. As I sit there thinking, I am often struck with a hilarious idea. I double up with laughter that resounds through the vacant rooms. I roll on the floor, banging my fists on my chest, kicking my feet about and often fracturing a toe. (I always try to think barefoot.)

When this subsides, I make my way upstairs to my study where I put one side of a white sheet of paper into my typewriter and then I forget what I was laughing about.

The average writer would go out and get drunk at this point. If he were more seasoned, he would stay home and get drunk. I do neither. I sit there and stare. After a while there slowly oozes up through the subconscious an idea that turns left at the occiput, takes the elevator to the midbrain and then springs out at me in full bloom.

At this point the telephone rings and a man wants to know if I have his shoes half-soled yet.

If you want to find out who is a writer of short humorous pieces you need only find a character whose telephone rings when he starts to work. If he has an earth-shakingly funny idea, the telephone is long distance from New York and consists of a hot tip on a Canadian uranium mine that will triple your money in three weeks. Will he put aside 5000 shares for you? No, he won't.

There is one more sign of the true humorous writer and that is that he has an intercom in his study and when he is doubled up with a great notion, his wife calls him on the intercom and wants to know if he has enough wool socks up there.

After all this is gone through, the writer takes the blank sheet out of the typewriter and puts in another one. The first one he would never again use. It is covered with wet tears, and anyway it is now totem. (Cf. Malinowski: *The Sexual Life of the Savages*)

If he is lucky and the rain doesn't beat down too hard on the roof and the doves don't coo too loud and the barometric pressure is right and the temperature is normal, the writer usually thinks of something amusing to write.

I hear you asking, "Where do you find the funny things to write?" This question often occurs to me so I have taken down from my valuable library a copy of a collection of "Post Scripts" from *The Saturday Evening Post* in which I appeared a number of times. Not often enough, maybe, but plenty.

The first piece I see by me is called "Letter from Camp" and that is just what it is: a letter from my oldest daughter in summer camp. I don't think I changed more than a dozen words, simply eliminating profanity and such. She was nine years old at the time and was developing the wrong type of vocabulary. Anyway, this piece ends, "We are studying crafts and Ferna started to make a bead bag but she is trying it on her feet now and maybe it will be a hat."

So there is one way to find funny pieces.

The next piece I see is "I Shall Have Music." This is devoted to an analysis of how it takes me three hours to play Chopin's "Minute Waltz" properly. (But when *I* get finished with it, it's *done!*) "Every note I play is clear and isolated. Lonely even." Well, this struck me as a funny notion because it is exactly how I *do* play the piano. I can read music, but I'm in no hurry to do it. I can read the various marks but it takes me a little time to do anything about it. I really enjoy playing the piano that way. For a long time it never struck me funny. Then one day it did. I wrote the piece. So one way to write a funny piece is to observe yourself carefully and see if there aren't some odd ways you have of doing things. My wife, for example, sticks her tongue way out and moves it in a semicircle when she's sewing. It looks very funny. I think she'd move it in a complete circle if it had ball bearings. Someday I'll write something funny about that.

The next piece in this volume of "Post Scripts" is "How to Finish a Table." This was at the height of the do-it-yourself craze, and I tried to take the finish off a table and put another one on. I am the world's worst do-it-yourself-er. In fact, I usually can't even find anyone to do it *for* me. Anyway, this piece told how I finished a table, and it ended up with my taking an axe and chopping it up. Then it was finished.

The next piece was called "Letter from a Fairly Unknown Woman" and again was a slightly edited note from one of my daughters announcing that she had decided to be a fashion model and was changing her name and would we please send her some mascara and a lipstick.

Another piece called "The Jolly Painters" described almost accurately my adventures while having three artistic characters, union members all, paint the interior of my house. It was all quite a mess. The painters were very sensitive and got eleven dollars an hour explaining how sensitive they were. I got back at them all with this little piece. Revenge is especially sweet when you get money for it.

Still another piece has to do with my reactions to a symphony concert. My wife used to insist on dragging me to concerts, which I abhor. I don't mind classical music in my own home where I can sleep comfortably, but public concerts upset me and give me a crick in the neck. I said as much in this piece and when my wife read it she turned red and never made me go to a concert again.

There is a piece here called "Household Hints." My wife went away to chaperone a beach week for my daughters' sorority and I was left all alone with the dishes. The result was quite an experience, which I later passed on to other lonely husbands. A couple of the hints are as follows and they are worth their weight in gold:

> Shorts and undershirts, after being washed, may be dried quickly by putting them on and going for a walk. They do not need to be ironed unless you are expecting the doctor.
>
> Wastebaskets can be used much longer if you get in them and jump up and down every day.
>
> If you do not put enough water in the rice when cooking it, you will have something else for dinner.

The final short by me in this volume is "What Ever Happened to Fathers?" My experience as a father was beginning to tell on me and I compared the days when I was a kid and my father was boss, to the days when I was the father and I had to get up and give the kids the comfortable chair. It seemed unfair. It still does.

Maybe all these things did not reduce you to fits of laughter. That is because everyone does not laugh at the same things. This is what you are up against in writing humor for magazines.

I used to write for radio and TV comedians, and when you write for them you normally do not have to worry about the audience laughing. You just spell out the joke in big letters for the comic to say and he says it. After that you write, (LAUGHTER). This means the audience laughs. A big neon sign lights up and says, LAUGH. If you don't, some of the younger men from the advertising agency walk through the aisles and horsewhip you. If you are an outstanding offender you may be banished from TV audiences forever. In that tribe, it is tantamount to death.

Of course, if you are at home listening or viewing and you don't think something is funny, you may write a letter to the station. This will do you no good because all letters are in the charge of chimpanzees, and the odds are astronomical against one of them even addressing an envelope properly.

On the other hand, when you write for a magazine there is no one to beat the reader into submission. He reads your piece, and if he doesn't chuckle you're sunk. You can't flash lights in front of him or explain to him or try something else.

All right, suppose we try to put down some easy-to-remember rules about writing short humor. First, though, let us list possible places to find ideas.

1. *Serious Magazine Articles.* Magazines these days are all full of malarkey about how to be beautiful, how to get rich, how to be nervous, how to build your own scaffold and all that stuff. Sometimes just reading an article like that aloud makes you laugh, and you can see that a little distortion here and there would make a funny piece. I once read an article by Marilyn Monroe on "How I Keep Beautiful." I wrote an article on how *I* keep beautiful. I used almost the same ideas as Monroe only on me they looked funny because while we both had the same measurements we had them in different places.

2. *The Inverted Idea.* This follows from #1. You read an article or piece about how to be rich or how to diet and then you invert it. You do something about how to be poor or how to get fat. Or, you turn the thing inside out. For example, while I have been sitting here doing nothing, I have been making notes for a piece about diets for, say, *Playboy.* This will consist of several diets for he-men and philanderers. What about a liquid diet consisting entirely of Scotch? People should eat stretched out flat so the food can disperse to the ends instead of settling in the middle. And so on.

3. *The Personal Problem.* All of us have problems of love, home, family and parental duty. They are serious problems, but when one of them is settled, it is well to look back in laughter. I have often left a bitter quarrel with my wife, walked upstairs with a piece of beefsteak to my eye, and then begun to see the humorous side of the thing. I recall once being able to get a piece out of it on "How To Understand What a Woman Is Talking About." I also did another called, "You Keep Talking But What

Are You Saying?" It is best not to show these pieces to your wife.

My children have also suggested funny articles. Recently I had a letter from my daughter in college complaining about the food, the strict housemother, the lack of boys, and so on. I wrote *her* a letter complaining about the food at home, the strict wife, the lack of well-stacked chicks, and the way all the other fathers had Jaguars and I had a beat-up Chevy. The letter, with some minor editing, made a good little piece.

4. *The Academic Drivel.* I usually write these shorts after reading a long, tiresome book on psychoanalysis, anthropology or economics. The gag here is to use the vocabulary and attitude of scholars in writing about commonplace affairs. I did a successful article on a feud with my neighbor, couching it in terms of diplomatic notes and foreign affairs commentators. I have often done pieces about weddings, birthday parties, and love affairs from the standpoint of an anthropologist. Psychotherapy offers many opportunities of explaining obvious things in a funny way by getting involved as hell with Freudian jargon.

5. *The Burlesque.* Exaggeration of solemn attitudes to the point of absurdity creates burlesque. An example was an article I wrote called, "I Was a Teen-Age Werewolf in Cairo's Sexy Alleys!" This was a gross parody of all the he-man stories about white slavery, hand-to-hand combats with sharks, army ants, and heaven knows what else.

6. *Statistics.* We live by statistics. You can hardly open a newspaper without reading that 11% of the American people sleep with one foot on the floor; that ten years after graduation the average Yale man has 1½ children.

Statistics are absurd because they never provide the truth about anything, and yet they claim to. The death rate of kangaroos is almost on the same curve with the increase in cigarette smoking in America. Are we permitting kangaroos to smoke too many cigarettes? It is an easy trick to take up some set of statistics and draw valid but nonsensical conclusions from them.

7. *Irrelevancies.* You can think these up by yourself. It is only necessary to start an apparently serious essay and then go wandering off in all directions. "How About Our Policy in Utria?"might be a good title, and then you can invent authorities who claim we are shipping too many bolts to Utria, providing an imbalance of nuts, thus lowering the output of ingots, and so on.

8. *Modern Complexities.* Great fun can be had from the fact that man has swept ahead scientifically a lot faster than he has intellectually. The result is he is a neurotic child playing with baffling toys he made with his own Erector Set #7. There are the vending machines that, when you want hot coffee, give your feet a massage. There are space rockets that have gone down instead of up, making a hell of a hole in the ground.

There are all the gimmicks around the house that permit the homemaker long hours of leisure in which to see her psychiatrist. There are power tools which take on a life of their own and cut the legs off the table on which they are mounted. Modern life knows no limit to the number of comforting life-saving devices that are killing us. They cry out for humorous treatment.

There are hundreds of other divisions into which material for short pieces might fall. I have merely listed a few that came to mind as I was standing here in the cold shower. By pasting this book in your hat, you'll have a handy reference when you are stuck for something humorous to write about.

I suppose a lot of you are saying, "That's all very well, but we don't even know how to type up short pieces or how to mail them or anything. Shucks!"

Well, I'm going to make a brief list of the items that might confuse you along those lines and see if we can't get all confused together.

1. Write on one side of the paper. A lot of people want to write on two sides of the paper because there *are* two sides to the paper. This seems logical but it isn't. Take my word for it.

2. Use white bond paper about 16-lb weight. I don't know what 16-lb weight means either, but it means that paper is what you may use.

3. Enclose a self-addressed stamped envelope. The envelope you enclose should be large enough to put the manuscript in. If you enclose a self-addressed stamped envelope the editor will see you are modest enough not to be sure your ms. will be accepted. Editors like modest writers. They usually are willing to accept the minimum rate until they're ready for social security.

4. Whom should you address short pieces to? This has puzzled me for some time. I started out addressing: Short Feature Editor. The first feature editor I met was nine feet tall so I saw my error. Then I said, "Editor Shorts." They had no editor named Shorts. The closest they could come was Hibbs and that isn't very close. I finally chose "Edi-

torial Department: Short Features." This seems to work except that the rejections often come back with a note signed by Rose Framingpaugh, Associate Beauty and Hair-do Editor. I remember, and this is a fact, a short feature I addressed to the editor of *Esquire* many years ago. He wrote me in person that somehow or other he was afraid the charwoman had thrown the piece in the wastebasket, but they were going to reject it anyway. This was the oddest rejection I ever had but one. That was when the charwoman sent me back the piece and said she didn't think it was funny, would I try again.

5. How long should a short piece be? Well, short humorous pieces run from 150 words to maybe 500. Pieces of a thousand words are still short pieces, but they will have to be fairly brilliant to sell. It is awfully hard to be funny for more than five hundred words, as readers of this unlimited chapter have probably noticed. Pieces over a thousand words should be called "lighthearted," because what you have to do there is take a lighthearted approach to some serious matter. You can be mildly humorous but you can't use burlesque or satire or irony.

6. How many short pieces should you submit at once? That depends. No editor likes to get so many pieces from one writer at once that he can't lift them. Editors often judge manuscripts by weight, so be wary.

Finally, let me tell you all how I got started being a humorist. I do it because it seems to me a good way to have fun, to develop your style, and to find out something about your audience.

I began by writing letters to local newspapers. I tried to be funny in those letters. I took local or national happenings, and I wrote tongue-in-cheek letters about them. This started other people answering my letters in print, and it began friendships with a number of neighbors and fellow citizens who would say, "That was a very funny letter you had in the paper today." Or, "I didn't think that last letter of yours was as funny as the first two." In this way I began to be able to judge what my contemporaries thought amusing and what they didn't think amusing. It was awfully good training and, as I said, a lot of fun. I branched out after that and wrote letters to the New York and Boston papers, and this was good training, too. Eventually an editor wrote me, "Why don't you try some of your humorous stuff on the magazines?" That was all I needed!

And that is about all I have to say this evening. In fact I don't know why I should encourage competition. I'm having a hard enough time as it is. Frankly I don't quite know how I got into this. I don't want the Panama Canal *that* badly!

6

THROWING SOME LIGHT ON LIGHT VERSE

by RICHARD ARMOUR

It annoys me when people, including those who are (or were) good friends, refer to my light verse as "limericks" or "doggerel." Occasionally, it is true, I write a limerick, which is a five-line piece of verse with a special rhyme scheme. But more often I write in a more flexible form that permits me to work for variety and also leaves me free to write something as short as a couplet (two lines) or as long as a quatrain (four lines) or several couplets or quatrains.

The person who thinks of "limericks" as a synonym for "light verse" is ignorant of verse forms, and I probably should pity such a person rather than be annoyed. But as one who has studied and published light verse for more than forty years, I think I have a right to bristle when what

I have worked so hard over is called "doggerel," a degrading, disparaging word. One dictionary definition of "doggerel" is "a sort of loose or irregular verse." Another is "mean or undignified poetry."

Since my verse is short, as light verse should be, it might be more accurate to call it "pupperel." However I try in my writing and rewriting to justify its being called "light verse," a playful but polished kind of poetry that goes back to Chaucer. In this century it has been written best by such light versifiers as Arthur Guiterman, Samuel Hoffenstein, David McCord, Morris Bishop, Dorothy Parker, Phyllis McGinley, and Ogden Nash, to mention only a few. I admire the work of these writers and wish I could write as well.

The trouble with light verse is that almost anyone can write it, but only a few can write it well enough to get editors to buy it. To the extent that writing light verse depends on a special attitude toward life, a turn of mind, it cannot be learned by reading about it. To the extent, however, that it depends on skill, a turn of phrase or playfulness in rhyme and meter, it can indeed be learned. Great (or at least competent) writers from little aptitudes grow. Like poets, light verse writers are born—and made better.

I have said that light verse should be short. Here is one of my shortest:

SHORT DEFINITION OF MOST SPORTS

Exercise
In disguise.

A very short piece of light verse is often helped by a contrastingly long title. Here is another:

BRIEF OBSERVATION ON WASHING WINDOWS

> The side there's a spot on
> Is the side that I'm *not* on.

You will notice the two-syllable rhyme in the "spot on—
not on" couplet. Fresh, unusual rhymes add to the fun of
light verse. The serious poet would avoid them, because
they would pull the reader's attention away from the
poet's lofty thoughts and imaginative figures of speech.
But the light verse writer, lacking such things, calls attention to his playful rhyming.

I find that if I start with an unusual, polysyllabic rhyme,
I continue with it, and the rhyming may be more fun for
the reader than the idea. Here is a slightly longer piece that
I sold to *The Wall Street Journal,* and I think it was largely
because of the rhymes that it was salable:

OH, HORRORS!

> Horror movies don't much enlighten me.
> They do, however, manage to frighten me.
> They're full of happenings weird and miraculous
> And ghosts and monsters and horrible Draculas.
>
> The movie ended, I go to my beddy-bye.
> Which I stand for a moment slightly unsteady by.
> I'm only human, I'm not a Titan . . . .
> I go to sleep with my bedside light on.

In this verse about horror movies, I didn't depend entirely on rhymes. Rhymes alone, I realized, would not have
been enough. So I had a little more to say in the second
stanza. In a sense, I made into a very short story what began only as a statement. You will also notice that I pic-

tured myself as something of a coward—which happens to be the truth. The writer of humor, whether in verse or prose, frequently reveals some personal weakness. He must be willing to make a fool of himself, not a hero.

Before I move on to other matters, or meters, let me quote a piece, originally in *The Saturday Evening Post*, that has an internal rhyme ("aisle-smile" and "rare-pair") in each stanza as well as a double (two-syllable) rhyme. The surprise in the last line is probably the main thing, but it is enhanced by the rhyming. Here it is:

TO HAVE AND TOO OLD

The bride, white of hair, is stooped over her cane,
   Her faltering footsteps need guiding,
While down the church aisle, with a wan, toothless smile,
   The groom in a wheelchair comes riding.

And who is this elderly couple, you ask?
   You'll find, when you've closely explored it,
That here is that rare, most conservative pair,
   Who waited till they could afford it.

As you will see, I have quoted nothing longer than eight lines. Since light verse is mostly used to fill out a column where the prose does not quite reach the bottom of the page, or to break up an otherwise solid page of prose, or to lend variety to such a feature as the "Post Scripts" pages of *The Saturday Evening Post* or the "Pepper and Salt" box on the editorial page of *The Wall Street Journal*, eight lines is about the maximum you can sell. Occasionally you might get away with ten or twelve lines. Once I placed this nineteen-liner because it happened to fit into a long, narrow space:

COMMENT ON COWS

Cows
Do nothing but browse
And drowse
And now and then moo.
That's all they do.
Yet even while grazing
They aren't lazing.
Even while snacking
They aren't slacking.
If not illustrious,
They are inner industrious,
Making milk with all their might
With every bite,
Cream too,
With every chew.
I'd like it fine
Could I combine
In such measure
Business with pleasure.

Sometimes it is possible to put together a group of short verses on the same general subject and find a market for them as a change of pace, a kind of extended filler. I have done this for the travel section of *The New York Times,* for several of the in-flight airline magazines (a high-paying as well as high-flying market), and even for the Christmas advertisement of a large chain of department stores.

Light verse, being so short, uses up ideas at a frightening rate. After selling more than 6,000 pieces to about 200 different magazines and newspapers, I often think there is nothing left to write about. But, wonder of wonders, just when I have almost given up I get a sudden burst of new ideas. One thing that starts me off is a chance phrase, such as "out of the woods." This led me to write:

PROGRESS REPORT

I'm out of the woods at last, I say,
And at first it is quite a thrill,
Till I notice that though I am out of the woods
I'm also over the hill.

Another piece came after a visit to my doctor for my annual physical examination:

ON SEEING AN X-RAY PICTURE OF MYSELF

Although I've really never been
Entranced with my exterior,
I must admit I'm glad for skin,
My inside's so much eerier.

Ideas come to me, as they could to you, while working in the garden, while getting a snack out of the refrigerator, while being the host or a guest at a party, while watching TV, while taking a bath. It was this last that gave me the idea for a quatrain I sold to *The Saturday Evening Post*:

IN A LATHER

One of the things that I've tried quite hard,
But still haven't managed to cope with,
Is the cake of soap that's too thick to discard
But a little too thin to soap with.

When I was in the bathtub, I didn't have my notebook and pen with me, but I am sure I had them close by. At night they are on the table next to my bed. The rest of the time they are in a coat pocket. Ideas are fleeting, and I must set them down or they may be gone forever. Even when I am driving, I manage to scribble a few words while steering with one hand. When I come to a stop light I am able to write more fully, perhaps completing a quatrain.

Next to the doctor's office, I find church my most creative place. Usually my mind wanders, and what I write has no connection with the sermon. On one occasion, however, I wrote a piece of light verse after hearing a sermon our minister gave about the conscience. I can't remember what he said, but I remember what I wrote:

ON MY CONSCIENCE

My conscience is a small, weak thing,
Unhandsome, too. So be it.
I'm glad, unlike my nose and hair,
It's hidden deep within me where
My friends and foes can't see it.

You might think my minister would be annoyed with me, but he is not. He thinks I am taking notes on his sermons, and I am one of his favorites.

A good source of material for light verse is the newspaper. I am constantly looking for an item that isn't itself funny but can be developed into a piece that I hope some editor will think amusing. Consider this:

HARK, HARK THE THRUSH

A birdwatcher in Texas reports that thrushes are getting drunk from eating too much fruit. They become so tipsy that they are unable to fly.

The tipsy thrush, with heavy wings,
Is earthbound as unpinioned things,
And overcome by lush excesses
To stupid flapping retrogresses.

How different the human mammal,
Imbibing like a thirsty camel.
He still can't fly, poor wingless man,
But now at least he thinks he can.

In the above, as in most of the verses I have quoted, there is a little surprise or unexpected twist at the end. The last line is the nut on the cookie. Of course if the poem is very long, the last line will have to have plenty of punch, almost a knockout blow, or the reader will feel cheated. Ideally, a piece of light verse should be funny all the way, with a bit of a lift at the end. It should not depend too much on that last line.

Writing good light verse, good enough to beat out the competition, isn't easy. You must master the fundamentals of rhyme and meter so that your lines will scan properly and your rhymes are both fresh and exact. I long ago stopped using the "college-knowledge" rhyme because it is so obvious and shopworn. But I keep at hand, and suggest that you do also, such a book as Langford Reed's *The Writer's Rhyming Dictionary,* along with a thesaurus and other tools of the trade.

As I have suggested, technique is of special importance in light verse. Sometimes I think it is more important than the idea. Though ideally the idea should be fresh and the technique both correct and clever, I have occasionally run across a piece of light verse in which an old idea is treated in a new and unexpected way. Let me make one suggestion about ideas, however, or call it an idea about ideas. It is simply that, though you write about yourself and your family and everyday occurrences, what you write and have fun with should apply also to others and be recognized by them. In other words it should have universality.

This is not difficult. What brings writer and reader together is that both are human beings. And light verse is the playful treatment, using meter, rhymes, and well-chosen words, of the foibles and absurdities of this imperfect human race.

Finally, a few words about markets. Light verse is harder to sell today than when I started writing it. Such magazines as *The New Yorker, Better Homes and Gardens,* and *Family Health* rarely if ever use light verse as fillers. Once they were among my best markets. Other magazines, such as *Look,* with its "Look on the Light Side" page, have gone out of business—perhaps because they used my light verse instead of something better. Tastes come and go; editors come and go.

But there are still markets for light verse, and I think there always will be. Though *The Saturday Evening Post* is no longer a weekly, its "Post Scripts" has grown from one page to two pages, and is brimming with light verse. *Good Housekeeping* now has its "Light Housekeeping" page, which is mostly light verse. A steady market is "Pepper and Salt" in *The Wall Street Journal.* Light verse is also used by *The American Legion Magazine, The Rotarian,* and such regional magazines as *Westways.*

These are only a few. I suggest you keep up-to-date by looking at the market lists in *The Writer* and *The Writer's Handbook.* Above all, study the magazines. You may happen on one that uses no light verse but needs just the sort of thing you write to lighten its pages. I have found several, over the years, and in some instances have established myself with a regular light verse feature.

If you think lightly and write brightly, if you keep many pieces in the mail, if you are not discouraged, or discouraged only briefly, by rejection slips, you will find editors who will publish what you submit. There will be ups and downs, but light verse is here to stay.

Stay with it.

7

WRITING THE SHORT HUMOR ITEM

by DAN BENNETT

Humorist and television comedy writer

A Short Humor Item Do-It-Yourself Writing Kit consists of the following:

    1 typewriter
    1 table
    1 chair
    1 supply of paper and carbon
    1 supply of envelopes and stamps
    1 average I.Q.
    1 superlative of stubbornness and perseverance

Humor is a personal thing—different to each person—and the art of writing humor is not learned from a book. What *can* be learned from a book is the form to use to send humor to the marketplace, ideas about where to get ideas, the compilation of material, slanting for specific markets, selling the manuscript and, most important of all, the marketplace itself.

Since I would not presume to give instruction in the art of writing humor, what I can do is tell others how I write myself, in the hope that my methods and experience might be of some benefit. But in the final analysis, each person who writes any type of literary material at all must work out his own salvation. There are no magic formulas. *You have to do the creating and writing yourself!* Nobody can tell you how!

In the science of General Semantics, originated by the Polish engineer, Alfred Korzybski, there is a phrase used frequently: "inside your skin." Applied to the creation of humor, I take it to mean that many writers get only a surface appreciation or surface feeling of the humor involved when they write, and they do not concentrate on the subject enough; or they are not sufficiently interested to work and study to get the necessary feeling or understanding of the humor of a written line. Thus they cannot tell if something is funny or not.

By concentrating and studying humor over a period of time, all writers who are successful in this field come to have that unconscious "inside your skin" feeling. Humor writers who have acquired the necessary experience can look at a line and tell immediately if it has a chance or not. And, as far as the ultimate sale is concerned, they are right far more often than they are wrong. They don't have to stop and classify the humor as 1) a Silly Situation, 2) a Reverse, 3) a Cliché, 4) a Well-Known Expression, or one of the other countless classifications that some instructors apply to humor. Because they have a deep "inside the skin" feeling of humor, they know immediately if it is good or not. The mechanical process of classifying does not lend itself to the creative arts, especially during the period of creation. And since this "inside the skin" knowledge can be gained only by long study of what has been done in the field of humor, what is being done, and by actually doing it yourself, it follows that the compilation of material is important.

The short humor forms that I specialize in are the Epigram, the Anecdote, and the Cartoon Gag. Before each type is analyzed, here are some things that apply in general to all three types.

THE COMPILATION OF MATERIAL

Every writer of the short humor item should have a file of humorous material to use as a springboard for new ideas. This means saving and putting into a usable file any humor material that he feels will be helpful in his work. This might include published epigrams, jokes, anecdotes, light verse, magazine cartoons, comic strips, amusing essays, collections of jokes and gags, funny true experiences, or old magazines and books containing humor items. I like to save the humor pages from magazines, and when I get enough of them, have them bound with a hard cover, labeled on the outside as to contents. I then place them in my library for reference. I also use scrapbooks for filing short items such as epigrams and poetry. I am constantly on the lookout for old humor books and magazines because they are the best source for new ideas that I know of. Also, they are valuable for the study of types and techniques of humor written in the past.

A good file takes a lot of room, and material for it must be saved over the years to be of any value. Classify your material in a way that you can use it best. Each writer has a different technique and therefore uses his file in a different manner. But keep a file!

THE MARKETPLACE

Writers very seldom write for their own amusement. They write for one thing—money! And the money is in the markets and has to be pried loose. So it follows that, other things being equal, the writer who knows the most about the markets for his particular type of writing is the most successful.

For many years I have taken every writers' magazine that is published, for one purpose—the hope of picking up even one additional market for my writing. It is surprising how a relatively small and unknown market, found in an obscure listing, can be developed into a source of steady income because it is not well enough known to have too many submissions of material.

Each market should be studied carefully for its editorial policy. Get back copies of the magazines and study the type of humor they print, and soon a common denominator will emerge. Perhaps it's a family magazine which likes an anecdote or epigram that appeals to everyone in the family group. A man's magazine is not going to be interested in the bright sayings of children, but in something a lot more earthy. A woman's magazine is more interested in problems that confront women than in gags about sports and gambling. If submissions are made to a particular market without regard to its wants, the whole thing becomes a waste of the writer's time and money. *Learn the markets—and give each magazine the type of material it wants.*

Markets can also be created. There are thousands upon thousands of trade magazines and house organs in the United States. The trade magazine is published for the benefit of people working in a certain industry, such as insurance, groceries, etc. The house organ is a magazine published by a certain company to keep its employees informed of what is going on in the company, and some of these magazines use humor to break the monotony of their publications. A humor writer who is on his toes can convince an editor who uses no humor that he may gain reader interest by including a quarter, a half or even a full page of humor. Naturally this takes a sales campaign, but if the editor agrees to let the writer furnish all the humor, it's a campaign won.

There are also thousands of weekly newspapers in America that are potential customers for the short humor item. One writer I know secured a "chain" of twenty small-town newspapers as markets to whom he sold a quarter-page weekly humor column. Heaven knows how many letters he wrote, how many different small-town newspapers he approached, before developing that particular market for his wares.

Another thing that must be remembered is that the bigger the magazine, the more competition there will be from other writers. A beginning writer can protect his ego by submitting his material to smaller markets, with much more chance of success until he learns the ropes. In the main, manuscripts can sell only at their own level, and most writers are slow to learn, and often unwilling to believe, what that level actually is.

An experienced writer gets to the point where he will not consider writing any item that will not fit into one or more of his regular market categories.

There is no absolute gauge or guide. In a way, finding a place for what one writes is not unlike finding a job. It takes a lot of hunting around, and not infrequently takes a lot of luck as well, but in the long run, as we know, most people do find jobs.

THE EPIGRAM

An epigram is a grain of truth told in the twinkling of an eye. The epigram is a short idea, the distillation of many words and thoughts. A person doesn't have to read 5,000 words to arrive at the conclusion an epigram brings him to immediately. For instance:

"Times have changed. Our fathers and grandfathers never dreamed of getting anything more from the government than a few garden seeds." A few words tell the whole story. This short epigram spans three generations and brings to mind a myriad of thoughts, different to each reader.

Take this one: "A bachelor is a man who can put on his socks from either end." This epigram conjures up an immediate humorous picture, as well as many other ideas about bachelors. It acts as a springboard to "A bachelor is a man who can't put something down in his apartment without putting it down on something else," or "A bachelor is a man who has to know how to remove a coffee stain from a catsup stain from a white tablecloth."

One thought leads to another, and one epigram also leads to another. An epigram can be a play on words, a pun perhaps, if it's good enough, but since the epigram is concerned with words, the epigram writer should become word-conscious. He should enlarge his vocabulary by studying the dictionary. He should carry a notebook and pencil and write down words or combinations of words he hears that appeal to his sense of humor. He should read and read and read—anything he can lay his hands on—because he never knows where an idea for an epigram will come from.

When it comes to the form to use for sending the epigram to the marketplace, there is no standard. I cut a sheet of 8½ by 11 paper into strips 8½ inches wide and about 2 inches deep. In the upper left-hand corner goes my name and address, in the upper right-hand corner goes my file number, leaving enough room on the strip for the typing of one epigram up to three lines in length. Naturally all epigrams should be typed and a carbon copy kept for the writer's file.

There have always been a lot of arguments as to how many epigrams should go to an editor in one batch. I take the position that quality pays off more than quantity. I write my epigrams in longhand one week and type them the following week, thus giving them a chance to cool off in the interim. It's surprising how many that looked good when I wrote them don't look so good a week later. Thus, by throwing out the ones I don't think will have a chance, I manage to come up with ten epigrams for a batch, which I type and send out. Ten epigrams, together with the forwarding envelope and the self-addressed, stamped return envelope, will go through the mails for one first-class stamp.

On the back of each carbon of the batch of epigrams, I stamp the date it goes out and write the name of the magazine to which it is sent. If one epigram is held by a magazine for further consideration, a notation is made on the back of the carbon copy. If the epigram is sold, the date sold and the price paid go on the back of the copy before it is placed in my "Sold" file. In other words, the back of the carbon copy of each epigram carries the whole history of that particular epigram. If one is held and then rejected, I note this on the back of the copy because it might be possible to interest that same market a following year.

Nobody can tell you how to write an epigram. You have to write it yourself. Take some famous old proverbs and try to twist them around to come up with something funny or philosophical. Take some old clichés, some well-known expressions, some wisecracks, and play around with the wording. Add some new words, substitute other words, shorten or lengthen. Practice! Write! Study! The popularity of the epigram is increasing all the time and writing them pays off.

THE ANECDOTE

The anecdote is a humorous story of an incident, which means anything from a two-line joke up to a story of a thousand words. Study the markets, pay attention to the anecdotal word requirements of the various magazines.

The origins of the anecdotes which are published in leading magazines today are very obscure. Many of those which are printed regularly are merely old jokes, brought up-to-date by the inclusion of modern implements. Others are true happenings, made more palatable by some polishing of the punch-lines. Still others are vignettes which have a particular point to make.

Most magazines want anecdotes about people and everyday life that are funny and point up a certain moral. They aim for identification with their readers, which every branch of entertainment and publishing seems to think is important in this modern age. However, some magazines lean toward the screwball type of anecdote which is a fantasy of the imagination, the type of thing that is funny but could never happen.

Again, as in the case of the epigram, the only way to satisfy the markets is to study them carefully. Current and back copies of magazines show the type of humor they buy.

There is no standard form for sending the anecdote to an editor. I cut an 8½ by 11 piece of paper into two pieces 8½ by 5½. Name and address go in the upper left-hand corner, of course. I try to limit the length of my anecdotes to about 150 or 160 words, which will go comfortably on an 8½ by 5½ piece of paper. I send my anecdotes to market six in a batch, and including the forwarding and return envelope, they go for a single stamp with no overweight problem. As in the case with epigrams, on the back of the carbon copy of the anecdote go the date it goes to market, the market's name and any other pertinent information.

Anecdotes are created in several ways. They can be switched from other jokes, which is the most common way. They can be built backwards from a funny punch-line; they can be built on a true happening; and they can be created out of thin air by a good imagination. Again comes the reason for keeping a good file of jokes, epigrams, cartoons and anything else that's funny. Reading humor is one of the best ways to get ideas for new humor. Keeping your eyes open for funny situations in real life is a must, for the humorist has to be observant and see the humor in situations around him.

And when you sit down to write the anecdote, know your markets well enough so that you can slant your material to their wants.

THE CARTOON GAG

Everyone is familiar with the magazine cartoon gag that is so popular these days. But maybe everyone doesn't know that most of the cartoon gags are originated by cartoon gagwriters, sent to the cartoonist who picks the ones he wants, draws them up, sells them and then gives the cartoon gagwriter a percentage of the selling price of the cartoon. This percentage is never lower than 25% and can go as high as the individual deal makes it.

I divide all cartoon gags into three categories:

(1) The Literary Cartoon: A funny caption attached to a drawing with no action in it. The drawing is usually a couple of people talking, and the caption would stand by itself without the drawing.

(2) The Captionless Cartoon: The funny drawing which needs no caption to explain it. The whole meaning is in the drawing.

(3) The Blend: The cartoon adds something to the caption, and the caption adds something to the cartoon. This is the perfect magazine cartoon.

Naturally the latter two types are the most popular and the ones most in demand by cartoonists. There's a special form in which to send out cartoon gags.

They should be typed on 3 x 5 cards, with a carbon copy kept for the writer's file. In the upper left-hand corner of the card goes the writer's name and address. In the upper right-hand corner goes the writer's file number for the gag.

Then comes the Scene and Caption, so the submission looks like this:

<pre>
Dan Bennett   #3789
1111 Smith Road
Los Angeles, Calif.
Scene: Mother talks to another woman as her little boy
          with extremely long hair stands nearby.
Caption: "Junior's growing Mother a new wig, aren't you
          darling?"
</pre>

You can write to any cartoonist in care of any magazine in which his work appears and make arrangements with him.

Six 3 x 5 cards with gags on them can be sent out to the cartoonist in one batch, plus the self-addressed, stamped return envelope. A good thing to remember is that most of the leading cartoonists get hundreds of gags in the mail every day, and they don't like to read through a lot of junk. Keep your batches short and your gags good.

The biggest complaint that cartoonists have with beginning gagwriters is that all of their gags are old and have been done. A thorough study has to be made by the beginner of everything that's been done in the cartoon field so he won't repeat published gags. It follows that a file of old cartoons is a must, both for study and as a base or springboard to new ideas.

Cartoon gags should always be kept simple, with a minimum of characters in the drawing and a minimum of dialogue in the caption.

HINTS TO THE WISE

Always use a self-addressed, stamped envelope if you

want to get your material back from either an editor or cartoonist. Always put your name and address on each piece of material. Always type everything you send out.

*   *   *

Keep your items as short as you can. That's the way to make them sparkle.

*   *   *

Avoid anything repulsive or disgusting.

*   *   *

Avoid profanity.

*   *   *

Avoid anything offensive to any race, religion or color.

*   *   *

Keep your manuscripts clean and presentable. Retype them if they come back dog-eared or ragged.

*   *   *

When you once write something, send it out and forget about it, and concentrate on writing something else. Keep your items on the road. They don't have a chance of selling while lying in a desk drawer or in a filing cabinet.

*   *   *

Never throw away anything you have written and not sold. Put it away in your slush pile and when you get time, take it out and rework it into something salable. Times and editors change, and what isn't funny to them one year might be the next.

*   *   *

Don't get discouraged if you keep seeing the same names in magazines all the time. There is plenty of room for you. The reason the same names appear constantly is that those are the writers who have stuck with it—writing and learning as they go along. Remember, editors will buy anything if it's good enough.

*   *   *

Don't worry about magazines stealing your writing and then not paying you for it. Magazines will lean over backwards to be fair with you. They pay for what they use.

*   *   *

The best way to write humor is to have a steady job from which you derive an income. In your spare time you can free lance in the humor field until you are well launched. Then, and only then, is it advisable to relinquish your position.

*   *   *

There is no rule or law that will make you a writer of truly funny humor. A successful humorist must have a natural knack for humor and acquire technique through experience.

8

RHYME DOES PAY

by SELMA GLASSER

Figured by the word, probably the most lucrative kind of writing today is what I call rhyme.

I'm not a poet and I know it! However, by utilizing all sorts of simple "sound" techniques, I have managed to produce eye-appealing, pun-concealing, rhyme-revealing fillers in the form of terse verse, light verse, prize-winning rhymes and last lines for creative contests.

On countless occasions this almost juvenile-sounding rhyme has paid me fairly well and featured my by-line as well. I have written terse verse for *Alive* and also gave the column in this teen magazine a rhymed title: "Phraze Craze." The editor, who obviously caught the rhyme fever, introduced my offering in this way:

77

A NEW TREAT

Answer the following questions with two words that rhyme.
For example:
"What's a pink flower?"   Answer: *Rosy Posy.*

My list of ten included:

What's a hot house?	*Swelter Shelter*
What's a matchmaker?	*Knotter Plotter*
What's an unwed Santa?	*Single Kringle*

A family magazine bought another list of seventeen
similar items. This time, I entitled the piece "Rime Time."
It went like this:

WHAT WOULD YOU CALL—

A pigeon-toed Britisher?	*Knockknee Cockney*
A kidnapper of a stripper?	*Peeler Stealer*
A cheap nose job?	*Frugal Bugle*

Notice also the ridiculous touch of absurdity and
whimsicality which doubtlessly helped put these rhymed
writings across.

My light verses appear in *Good Housekeeping, Medical
World News, Saturday Evening Post,* etc. A recent one was
triggered by a news item I read which stated: " 'Daylight
Obstetrics' program begun ... babies delivered between
9 a.m. and 5 p.m. only," and my published poem (in *The
American Journal of Nursing*) went like this:

DAY LABOR ONLY

No longer need we wives be quivery
About a late or dawn delivery;
No more a sudden, quick emergency
Of instant, unpredicted urgency!
No labor paining to despair of
Or rousing spouses to take care of;

No summoning the obstetrician
For posthaste hospital admission.
No nights—just days—from 9 to 5,
That's when the babies must arrive!
But with my luck, I've got a hunch
My doctor will be out to lunch!

To illustrate further the popularity of humorous rhymes, here is an example of a simple piece of verse I wrote recently. It might possibly have made an amusing epigram because of its obvious but exasperating reality. However, when I put it into light verse, I believe it took on a bonus element, and it sold promptly to *Good Housekeeping* and appeared on its "Light Housekeeping" page.

DRIVER'S DILEMMA

I'm quitting traffic's "short cut" scene,
Which fills my daily driving cup;
Because the shortest distance between
Two points is usually torn up!

Sometimes, when I fool around with rhymes, I find that if I come up with an exceptionally punny title or take-off on an ordinary phrase, my light verse practically writes itself. Occasionally I use a second pun as the punch line to

the piece, if possible. Here is just such a poem that was
sold to *Today's Family:*

WEATHER FLAWCASTERS

Predicting weather, they're so wrong,
  With each and every scoop;
That's why forecasters all belong
  To a NON-PROPHET group!

Occasionally, as mentioned before, a phrase will almost
come begging to be used or converted into a pun or parody
expression. This has happened many times and resulted in
salable ideas for epigrams, light verse, titles, last lines, etc.
From problem drinkers I arrived at problem thinkers. This
is the poem that emerged, which was sold to *Family
Weekly:*

THE PROBLEM THINKERS

Advice on marriage, love or sex,
  These columnists provide;
They're clever, sensible and wise,
  And very qualified;
But, surely, problems cross their paths
  At home, where they reside —
I wonder where they turn for help,
  In whom do they confide?

In another instance, the common word *plastic* stayed in
my mind for a long time before I figured out what to do
with it. I heard a discussion on "plastic surgery" and an
idea took hold. What a humorous name to describe such a
delicate type of operation—if you think of the word
"plastic" in its ordinary, daily meaning. To emphasize my

point, let me give you an illustration of a piece of light verse that has no puns or out-of-the-ordinary cleverness. I simply expanded on the dictionary definition of an ordinary word (plastic). Except for that touch of whimsy which makes for good light verse, it is the straight statement of a double meaning long used in medicine. I wrote these lines and here is how Dr. Morris Fishbein in *Medical World News* presented it in his "Every Other Friday" column:

INDEX OF SUSPICION

Selma Glasser, who feels that man-made substances may become overemphasized, writes:

> Synthetic products sure are great,
>   But it would take some urgin'
> To get a gal like me to go
>   And see a plastic surgeon.

The hay fever season occurs with its agonizing regularity year after year. Unfortunately, I am one of its victims. Although this is no laughing matter, we writers do best on subjects that hit home or are familiar to us. In fact, one of the most infuriating sidelights of having hay fever is listening to daily television and radio broadcasts of pollen counts. During one siege of reaction to those noxious substances, I wrote and sold this two-liner to *The Saturday Evening Post* at the height of the hay fever season (and sneezin'):

POLLEN COUNTS

> Hay fever will eventually go,
> But usually, only blow-by-blow!

Notice, if you will, how I gave the term *blow-by-blow* its true connotation in this connection. The title "Pollen Counts" has double meaning.

Consider now the phrase *spring fever,* which usually occurs after a long hard winter and conjures up thoughts of young budding romance or laziness. Or does it? Not to this filler-writer! While nursing a temperature of 103, I got this idea which sold to *Good Housekeeping:*

SPRING FEVER

In spring life focuses,
On yellow crocuses,
Pots of blue irises,
And lots of new viruses!

While still suffering from my usual seasonal rhinitis, I recall reading about sit-ins, laugh-ins, etc. Here is the verse I wrote and sold to *Today's Family* shortly thereafter:

UPDATING RAGWEED

When hay fever pollen starts to "breeze-in"
Then united sufferers have a "sneeze-in!"

I also realized that talk about ecology is constantly on everyone's tongue. I thought about it for a while and came up with this take-off: "Eek-Ology"—and composed the following light verse—and breathed a lot easier when I placed it with *The American Journal of Nursing:*

EEK-OLOGY

I'd surely love to take deep breaths
But never dared to

Since learning of the many ills
That man is AIRED to!

Toying with the word "transplant" in its literal meaning
(while reading about the modern medical miracles that are
being accomplished), I got an idea for a verse. *Medical
World News* liked it and published it:

VITAL ORGAN RECITAL

My heart is a-quiver
I offered my liver,
My lungs or a kidney,
Go on, you can rid me
Of prime parts for transplanting;
My permission I'm granting!
But would it be dull, sir,
To offer my ulcer,
A disc that is slipping,
Or nose which keeps dripping,
Ugly veins which are showing,
Legs that pain and are slowing?
I offer my used parts,
My much more abused parts;
A trade-in would please me,
You might even freeze me,
Then change parts-a-plenty,
Until I feel twenty!

To sum up, light verse can incorporate timely, topical or
perennial happenings—be they seasonal, medical, or prob-
lematic. The important thing is to make light of familiar,
recognizable events, and gently poke fun at institutions
and situations. In short, we might as well "grin" as we bear
it!

9

CRACKING THE QUIP

by RICHARD ARMOUR

The shortest of all the short forms of writing is the quip—also known as the epigram, the aphorism, the saying, the saw, the wisecrack, the filler, and the quote. There may be a little difference between the quip or wisecrack and the epigram or aphorism, because the former is likely to be humorous and the latter wise. But humor and wisdom are, in my opinion, akin. A wise saying can be funny and a funny saying can be wise. Both involve either witty twisting of language or sharp perception of human nature, or both.

It has always seemed to me that there is a relationship between the I.Q. and what might be called the H.Q., or Humor Quotient. People who are slow to catch a joke are likely to be slow to catch anything, except maybe a cold. Certainly the smartest characters in Shakespeare's plays are some of his clowns and fools, and if the kings had listened to their advice, they would have been alive at the end of the fifth act.

So there is a certain amount of wisdom, or at least human understanding, in a good quip. Moreover, it is a type of writing, the ultimate in condensation, which has a long and honorable history. It goes back to Confucius, the morals at the end of each of Aesop's Fables, and the memorable sentences, good enough to stand alone, in the essays of Montaigne and Bacon. The French have excelled at the brief, witty, quotable epigram, but Americans have done well with the writings of Benjamin Franklin, Mark Twain, Ambrose Bierce (notably in *The Devil's Dictionary*), and Will Rogers, to name a few.

Mention of Aesop brings to mind James Thurber and two of his books, *Fables for Our Time* and *Further Fables for Our Time*. Like Aesop, Thurber concludes each of his fables with a "Moral." For example: "It is better to have the ring of freedom in your ears than in your nose" and, playing with words as well as ideas, "It is wiser to be hendubious than cocksure." I followed the good example of Aesop and Thurber in *It All Started with Eve,* where I have a "moral" after my playful account of each of thirteen famous women, from Eve to Mata Hari. For instance, the moral with which I conclude the story of Helen of Troy is "Beauty is only skin deep, and the world is full of thin-skinned people."

I have said that the quip (and I shall henceforth use the shortest of the several terms mentioned above) is the shortest of all the short forms of writing. How short is short? Well, a quip is rarely longer than one sentence, and it may be not more than a verbless phrase. Calculated by the word, it is probably the most lucrative kind of writing today, for a quip will usually bring ten dollars from any of the better magazines. A ten-word quip would thus pay the writer a dollar a word. A five-word quip would bring the rate up to two dollars a word. Reprints may multiply this figure many times over, though there is a tendency for quips not only to be used again without payment, but to be used without the author's name, or with someone else's name. "It's a wise crack that knows its own father," as someone (you see I don't know who) once quipped about the quip.

Since the quip brings so much for so little, it would seem that one could quickly get rich by sitting down and writing maybe a hundred quips a day. But, though quips to some extent can be manufactured, they cannot be turned out at any such rate, or not for long. It is an odd thing, but for five or six years I rode high on a wave of quips. All I had to do was to push my brain around for half an hour and I would produce six or eight. Before the vein, or the artery, wore out, I had written more than two thousand, a good proportion of which I sold and many of which were reprinted in *The Reader's Digest.*

But suddenly I got so I could push my brain for an hour, push it until it was out of shape, and produce maybe one quip or half a quip (a half-witticism) or none at all. Nowadays a quip comes occasionally, if I work hard enough at it, but I seem to have lost the ability to produce on a large scale. Perhaps there is a fruitful season, a time when quips are hanging there, ripe for the picking. Then the frost comes. But maybe what is needed is a new, untired picker—such as you.

Yes, your mind may be just at the state when, if you stir

it around a little, or shake it, the quips will start dropping as they once did for me and as they may again. There is a large demand for quips, which fill in the small spaces in a magazine and are used up fast. Some of the magazines using them are *Family Weekly,* for its "Quips and Quotes" section; *Quote,* which provides one-liners as well as slightly longer pieces for public speakers; and the widely read "Pepper and Salt" feature on the editorial page of *The Wall Street Journal.* Markets are as various as the *American Legion Magazine, The Rotarian,* and *Good Housekeeping,* to mention only a few. But their needs change, and you must keep watching these magazines closely.

Probably the best paying and most widely read magazine using quips is *Reader's Digest.* Usually it reprints quips from other magazines, but I know from personal experience that it sometimes takes quips sent to it directly.

How to get started at quip writing? One thing you might do is to look at quips that have been published, carefully study the successful product. Some 30,000 quotations, many of which are the type that might be called quips, may be found in H.L. Mencken's *New Dictionary of Quotations.* A handier collection is Frederick B. Wilcox's *A Little Book of Aphorisms.* An ingenious, dictionary-arranged mass of quips with higher humor content and less literary value is Evan Esar's amusing *Esar's Comic Dictionary.* And not to be overlooked is Leonard Louis Levinson's irreverent and impertinent *Left-Handed Dictionary,* the result of thirty years of collecting witticisms and adding some of his own.

In addition to leafing through these collections, it would be a good idea to examine current magazines, both to look at models and to study markets.

A special reason for reading others' quips is that these will frequently furnish the starting point for one's own. Many modern quips are merely new twists of familiar sayings, common expressions, clichés. What one does is to start with the known and try to emerge with something unexpected but still plausible, as well as both wise and amusing. See what has been done, for example, with the age-old observation, an antique but not antiquated quip, "People who live in glass houses shouldn't throw stones." Under *glass houses* Esar lists several variations on the theme, including "People who live in glass houses shouldn't throw parties" and "People who live in glass houses shouldn't." The first of these, which continues the familiar saying but in an unexpected direction, might be described as a "twisted cliché." The second, which ends abruptly before the saying is concluded, and yet makes sense and brings out a new meaning, might be called a "truncated cliché." To these should be added the "extended cliché," in which the common expression is neither twisted nor cut, but is carried on to an entirely new conclusion. An example of this is "Cleanliness is next to godliness, but in children it's next to impossible."

I can't get that "People who live in glass houses" saying out of my mind. I have just thought of another twist: "People who live in stone houses shouldn't throw glasses."

An amusing example of what can be done with the truncated cliché is a quip (the source of which I cannot place) in which, by cutting off but a single letter, the author brought out a fresh and possibly appropriate meaning. The one I am thinking of is: "Having a wonderful time. Wish you were *her.*" An example of a twisted cliché in which only one word is altered is: "Many hands *want* light work." Or, with reference to bureaucracy and Parkinson's Law, it could be: "Many hands make work." So also: "A watched pot never boils over."

The last one is perhaps more nearly an extended cliché, although it is extended by only one word. This is my favorite kind of quip, the kind I write most often. Thus a bit of thought on "a man's man" gave me "A man's man is very often a woman's too," which was taken by *Ladies' Home Journal.* The expression "to carry a tune," having gone through the converting and perverting process of my mind, led me to the observation that "Some people can carry a tune, but they seem to stagger under the load." This was used as a filler in *The Saturday Evening Post.* The same magazine also took "When it comes to eating, you can sometimes help yourself more by helping yourself less" and "People who are really bright do a lot of reflecting."

Word play, as in the above, can also be the basis of a piece of light verse, providing either the idea or the clincher at the end. So it is not surprising that what I first jotted down as a quip may eventually come out instead as the last line of a quatrain. As Shakespeare almost said, "The word play's the thing."

Quips often take the form of definitions, though not quite the sort found in a serious dictionary. The prevailing tone is usually cynical; the wit or humor derives from incongruity between the lofty or at least respectable word and the crass, realistic "definition" of it. In America, Ambrose Bierce was one of the early masters of this technique. A little later came the sharp-penned H.L. Mencken. Consider Bierce's definition of "to be positive," which he says is "to be mistaken at the top of one's voice." Or

Cracking the Quip

Mencken on "hope"—"A pathological belief in the occurrence of the impossible"; and "immorality"—"The morality of those who are having a better time."

But most of the definition-quips are anonymous; for instance, "Diplomat: A man who remembers a lady's birthday but forgets her age," and "Expert: An ordinary man away from home giving advice." One of mine, with a little word play thrown in, is "Agreeable people are people who agree with you." Another is "Adolescence is when children start trying to bring up their parents." Cynicism is generally but not always the rule. The definition-type quip can also be written pretty straight, and with an element of the figurative or poetic, as in "A gossip is a woman who warms herself by the fire of other people's burning ears," or "Wisdom is knowledge that has been cured in the brine of tears."

So many humorous definitions begin "A woman is . . ." that a quip might almost be defined as "A short saying which begins 'A woman is . . .' " But other favorites are "Middle age is . . ." and "The good old days were when . . ." Again, you might say: "The good old days were when nobody referred to the good old days."

Definition-quips have sometimes been strung together to make an entire book, as in Ambrose Bierce's *The Devil's Dictionary*. More often they are included, along with other types of humor, in such an anthology as *The Reader's Digest Treasury of Wit and Humor,* put together by the editors of *The Reader's Digest.* The quips are grouped in such categories as "Quotable Quotes," "Variations on a Theme," and "Deft Definitions." I am happy to be included in all of these, an example being my "Adolescence isn't a period; it's a coma."

Once I compiled a short magazine feature which was made up of quips of mine that had not been previously published. It was called "Definitions Not in the Dictionary":

Balanced diet: what you eat at buffet suppers.

Bookkeeper: a person who fails to return the book you lent him.

Buckshot: what a dollar is, these days, after you have bought something.

Capital punishment: spending the summer in Washington, D.C.

Climate: weather that has got into a rut.

Dogma: a mother dog.

Friendly argument: one that has just started.

Gossip: a person to whom no news is bad news.

Picture hat: a hat worn by a woman in front of you at the movies that keeps you from seeing the picture.

Sweater girl: a girl who makes the men tend to her knitting.

Trade secrets: what women do.

Turkey gobbler: a person who eats lots of turkey.

Vacation bound: what you are for the rest of the year after you have paid for your vacation.

Waiter: a person who jealously guards the restaurant's water supply.

Frequently a quip involves an original sort of comparison or differentiation. What is called for, in the first instance, is a fresh and colorful simile in which there is an essential, if somewhat exaggerated, likeness between the subject and the thing with which it is compared. Thus Don Marquis, remembered best for his *archy and mehitabel,* is credited with the oft-quoted: "Publishing a volume of verse is like dropping a rose petal down the Grand Canyon and waiting for the echo." Or consider the anonymous "A good speech, like a woman's skirt, should be long enough to cover the subject and short enough to create interest."

A still more fertile field is the sort of quip that starts out, "The difference between ..." Among the quips of this type I have written are: "The difference between shortsightedness and nearsightedness is that nearsightedness is correctible"; and, with perhaps a little more surprise: "The difference between playing golf for the game and for the exercise is about ten strokes." However grotesque the comparison, the completed statement should make sense, and also be unexpected.

While a quip may contain word play, or even such a coinage as "break-a-brac" or "Santa Claustrophobia," it will get along very nicely if it is simply a wise observation about life, stated succinctly. Balanced phraseology may help, as in Oscar Wilde's "It is better to be beautiful than to be good, but it is better to be good than to be ugly." For my own part, I have managed to ring the editorial bell with such simple truisms as: "It is easy for people who are not hungry to have good table manners"; "When people say they are giving you their opinion for what it is worth, you can be sure they are putting a high value on it" (in which will be recognized a trace of the extended cliché); and "There is some consolation in the fact that, even though your dreams don't come true, neither do your nightmares." One that combines homespun wisdom with word play and surprise ending is: "Every young man has two good openings—his ears." But the important thing in all of these is the common sense content.

The idea need not be new—in fact I sometimes wonder whether a wholly new idea is possible any more. Rather, it should be a universally accepted thought which is stated with new force and compression. As Dr. Johnson, a lexicographer and an expert quipster himself, once stated about aphorisms, a quip consists "not so much in the expression of some rare or abstruse statement as in the comprehension of some obvious and useful truth in a few words." It follows that the subjects of quips must be those of general and everyday interest: love, money, youth and age, politics, health, religion, friendship, success, and so on.

To illustrate the variety of quips, here are a few of the good, bad, and indifferent ones from my files:

Some speakers cover a subject so thoroughly that you can't see a trace of it.

A sweeping statement can raise a lot of dust.

You can have your close friends; give me generous ones.

When a man hasn't a leg to stand on, he is likely to make some lame excuses.

Some of us might care for pets more if we didn't have to care for them so much.

In a traffic accident, the one who is right is not always the one who is left.

The man who divorces a talkative wife and remarries may just be getting his second wind.

To the pessimist, some people are born lucky; to the optimist, everyone is lucky to have been born.

Tact is the art of saying what you think only when it is what others wish to hear.

Some people have a hard row to hoe, and no hoe.

To the insomniac, it's a great life if you don't waken.

The shoe shine boy is one fellow who makes money hand over foot.

When youth burns the midnight oil these days, it is usually in the crankcase.

Some people make spectacles of themselves with a couple of glasses.

Of the above quips, some were sold and some were not. If you can tell which are which, you may have the makings of a quip writer—or an editor.

Short as it is, and perhaps because it is so short, a quip takes even more polishing than most kinds of writing. Extraneous words must be deleted. Weak words must be replaced by more precise or more colorful words. Unless the quip is too timely to keep, you might well let it settle and ripen with age. Although it cannot improve of itself with time, the writer may, with time, see that it needs improving, and discover how to improve it.

As for submitting quips, they can be typed individually, one to a sheet of paper. Or they can be submitted several on a page, with enough space between them so that the editor may, if he accepts one, clip it off and return the rest. But this in unimportant. A really good quip will shine through any wrapper. The main thing is to write lots and lots of them. With quips, as with the years, the first hundred are the hardest.

10

AN EDITOR'S VIEWPOINT

by GURNEY WILLIAMS

Former humor editor of a national magazine

If someone offered me two dollars to dream up the equivalent of the businessman's *Think* sign for humorists, I'd suggest *Restraint,* for the reason that the outstanding weakness of material I rejected is overemphasis. Writers I have known take the "Boy, am I funny!" approach, trying to overcome an editor's steadfast resistance to the bombastic and wearisome clown of letters.

Let's begin with a simple thing like the exclamation point. Many professionals and most amateurs seem to feel that the liberal use of ! ! ! ! !s will punch up flagging material. For me, exclamation points shout too much, like the baggy-pants, loud-mouthed comedians of burlesque. The better humor markets are not media in which screaming comics are regarded with favor.

Here's an epigram as it might be written by a "bang-point" enthusiast: "Life can be very unpleasant when you get into the 80's, especially if a motorcycle cop is following you!" If that last punctuation mark makes it funnier, wouldn't two of them make it even more amusing? Obviously not. Restraint, the low-key treatment, is far more effective.

This is not to imply that the exclamation point is obsolete. It can, for one thing, create a sense of enthusiasm necessary for a certain type of characterization, as in the following item from a series of sketches titled, "There's No Use Getting All Steamed Up."

> "Listen, Harry; I just put in a complete stereophonic outfit and it's out of this world! Two 50-watt Woofle-Craft amplifiers, matching 12-inch coaxial Wow-Audio speakers and a Tweet-Sound pickup arm on a Flutterberg turntable! You ought to hear *Rachmaninoff's Second Concerto* on this rig! Fantastic!"
>
> To which Harry says simply:
> "My hobby is stamps."

The exclamation points enable us to feel the hi-fi enthusiast's fanaticism; we can almost hear his excited recital. In contrast is the stamp collector's flat statement.

Immoderate use of italics, too, can trip an unwary humor writer. In the following epigram the italics are superfluous but could easily have been used by a humorist who makes too much of a point of making a point. "An old-timer is a man who once was a celebrity *because he won $100 on a quiz program.*" The same goes for capital letters. You might call it unnecessary impact.

This tendency to accentuate the obvious—the "ha, ha, get it?" business—does not improve a flimsy idea and only weakens a good one. Perhaps it might be well to keep in mind that your reader is not an oaf who must have everything explained to him. Consider him to be your peer in intelligence; let the slow-witted character spell things out if he must.

What do you write, or want to write—epigrams, light verse, short prose humor, all three?

If you have a flair for both epigrams and verse, one can be played against the other. That is, a pungent comment, or epigram, can often be stretched into a poem (and a bigger check). One of my tests for a piece of verse is to ignore the rhyme formation and see if the bare idea stands on its own feet. The result is what I call Williams' Law: "If a four-line poem can be rewritten as an amusing epigram, it's a sound quatrain, and vice versa." Let's see how this checks out.

Epigram: We know a lot of suburbanites who have discovered that trees grow on money.

Verse: The country dweller's one who knows
(To him, this isn't funny)
The dough he spends on saplings shows
That trees do grow on money.

Conversely: There's one sure thing:
Your phone won't ring
And disturb a deserved slumber,
If you have a son
Under twenty-one,
Who calls up a real cool number.

Epigram: If you want to keep the phone from ringing while you take a two-hour nap, just ask your teen-age daughter to call up one of her friends.

However, if the transition from one form to another seems contrived, don't labor over it; stay with the original construction. The free-and-easy bit is generally more successful.

As a verse buyer, I found that writers too often depend upon a clever rhyme scheme to bolster a limp idea, or no idea. Rhyming the last words in every line is a favorite experiment which goes like this:

> I tore my pants
> On thorny plants
> And my wife rants
> At my expanse.
> I'm glad the ants—

—and so on, usually to nowhere.

There's a place for contrived *words* in rhyme, though, not only because the improvisations themselves can be funny but because they give the writer a lot of latitude. "Hi-Fi Ho Hum" was the title of this three-liner:

> I wish so
> That calypso
> Would collapso.

A professor of English might go mad trying to scan this doggerel but it appealed, nevertheless, and was quoted on TV and radio following its appearance in print.

A two-line bit that read:

> Relatives with cameras
> Seldom make you glameras

wound up as a one-line item in *The Reader's Digest* "Picturesque Speech" department minus the title—"The Old Focus at Home"—itself a somewhat pasty gem.

As a rule, a legitimate word like cameras should precede "glameras," which is really no word at all and might distract the customers. They must be conditioned, made receptive, to the unorthodox. If a reader stumbles over a two-liner reading:

> A lot of girls aren't glameras
> Before the TV cameras

he's apt to get irritated and you'll never get famous.

The indestructible pun will, as you probably know, always find a market. Use puns wisely; don't let them use you. Some of your friends and mine verbally overdo this form of humor to the point of intolerable boredom. They'll interrupt a conversation just for the sake of making a pun, whether it's pertinent or not. Usually, it isn't. This failing can beset a writer, too. Again, the *Restraint* sign.

Comments on the news have a place in the "filler" category, and puns can give them an added lightness. Consider these (the comments are set off here in parentheses):

> In Mobile, Ala., a hen flew into the tax collector's office and laid an egg. (The ordinary taxpayer does this only when he is called in to explain a deduction.)

> Two pilots demolished their light plane near Lupin Lodge, Calif., after skimming the tree-tops of a nudist camp. (Contrary to accepted flying procedure, it's obvious they should have been less attentive to the take-off and avoided the strip altogether.)

The National Macaroni Institute estimates that every American ate an average of 25,000 inches of spaghetti last year. (This obviously does not include yardage lost by incomplete passes.)

From experience, I've learned not to mull over any news item that isn't inherently humorous or does not lend itself easily to a quick quip. Here's a straight one, with no pun needed:

The Soviet Union claims to have produced a camera capable of taking 32,000,000 pictures a second. (Having just viewed our neighbor's vacation slides, we feel pretty certain this invention has been around for some time.)

The subject of news items brings us to the question of timely and topical humor. (Here I use the first definition of the word topical: "pertaining to place.") Timely humor can't be handled well in the big-circulation magazines because of the time lag between the creation of the piece and its appearance, five to eight weeks later, on the newsstands. The eternal problem of both writer and editor is to try to determine which of today's events will survive the hiatus.

As to topical affairs, editors of national magazines know there are a lot of readers in Fargo, Fairbanks, Fort Dodge and Filadelfia who don't give a fig about what's hot in, say, Manhattan. A writer, likewise, must avoid provincial thinking, no matter where he lives. This means simply that humorous material must relate to experiences common to the greatest possible number of readers. *The New Yorker* is tops in its field; yet many of the best cartoons and comments, based purely on metropolitan New York situations, are often incomprehensible to the most astute of its out-of-town readers.

This basic premise applies, of course, to all forms of humor. When an idea calls for straight exposition, or narration, make sure the subject matter is of wide interest. If your essay concerning the eccentricities of your grandfather is rejected by every editor in the business, try to look objectively at what seemed to be a "natural." The fact that your grandfather may have had an uncommonly peculiar habit is, to be sure, hilarious to you and your family, but you may find it impossible to amuse your readers with an account of it. They could more easily feel sympathetic toward your grandfather if you told them about his contempt for modern inventions, or the irritations he experienced with any of the facets of living that irritate almost everybody. The three F's—human frailties, foibles and frustrations—make up the meat of the matter. Concentrate on them and you'll *communicate.*

Note the simplicity of this episode, which was published under the title, "How to Open Your Big Yap in Public":

All of us occasionally find ourselves in tight little embarrassments which call for an appropriate remark. But under stress, we generally find ourselves at a loss for words. You needn't be tongue-tied. Just memorize the simple sentences you'll find in my book called *Crushers.* They've been tailored to fit all the usual situations. Page 86 contains this example:

While driving in traffic, you signal for a right turn but make a left turn by mistake, and a large truck crashes into your fender. The driver—a huge man with cauliflower ears—descends from his cab and lumbers toward you. A crowd gathers.

"Well?" growls the truck driver belligerently. Taking the initiative, you stare steadily at him, and in a loud and even voice you say: "Since when did they start issuing driving permits to mentally retarded orangutans?" There will be a roar of laughter from the bystanders at your sally. This will be followed immediately by a round of applause as the truck driver breaks your nose.

The price of the book is $2.95 and all sales are final.

Following publication of this piece, one reader confessed with some chagrin that he had asked a book dealer for a copy of *Crushers* and had been told it didn't exist. From this I gather (1) that he liked the item enough to want more, or that (2) he had no sense of humor and was taken in by the restrained treatment.

Here, in part, is another way of handling similar everyday annoyances. This was called "Letters I Have Drastically Revised":

Dear County Utilities:

I have your card notifying me that the gas and electric rates have been raised 60 cents per month. This is an unmitigated outrage. Kindly shut off the service at my residence and have the meters remov—

Dear Director of Internal Revenue:

Your letter requesting me to appear at your office bearing proof of contributions claimed in my 1976 return strikes me as being a pretty imperious demand from a government employee. As a taxpayer, I feel my civil liberties are endangered, and I flatly refu—

This type of subject matter offers unlimited possibilities and can be presented in many forms.

Short pieces written entirely in dialogue make for easy reading, but dialogue is a tricky commodity. Tyros, especially, have trouble with quotes, and a great deal of supposedly funny conversation reads too awkwardly to be credible. Here's a little horror: "What's that, officer? You say I was doing 75 and you're going to give me a ticket? Well, look at that sign there. It says '75.' Oh—that's the route number?" I'm not exaggerating much; I see even more stilted writing every day.

Assuming you do not find dialogue cumbersome, short conversational sentences, headed by a covering title, are fairly easy to write; but this device has been worked over a great deal and can become static unless one's ingenuity and imagination are fully utilized. You've seen a countless number of such pieces titled, "Things I Wish I Had Said Instead," "Questions I Shouldn't Have Asked" and the like. For example, here in toto is "Honesty Is a Tough Policy":

It has been a lovely evening, but I'm afraid we've stayed much too long."
"You sure have."

*   *   *

"Well, it turned out to be acute appendicitis and the doctor said—but I don't want to bore you."
"Then why do you?"

*   *   *

"So after I finished telling Johnny about the birds and the bees, do you know what he said?"
"No, and I hope I never find out."

*   *   *

"I know I'm not pretty. There are lots prettier girls than me."
"I agree with you."

*   *   *

"That was *Moonlight on the Ganges*. Not bad for only two lessons, was it?"

"It was the most atrocious guitar playing I've ever heard."

*   *   *

"Tell me honestly: Do you think I have a sense of humor?"
"No."

Since there is no real beginning or ending to such pieces, it is wise for the writer to dream up more items than a magazine would ordinarily use. This gives the editor a choice and the script can easily be cut (without hurting the piece *or* the writer) to fit a niche on a page which couldn't accommodate a tightly written essay. It might even be split into two parts and run in successive issues.

There was a vogue, many years ago, for the suprise-ending technique, the function of which was to upset the premise the writer led the reader to build up. You remember: "He stroked her long, silky hair and whispered, 'I love you, Geraldine.'" This went on for 300 words until we reached the snapper: The subject was a pet cat. It's difficult to fool today's readers, but it can be done. Here are two that did the trick.

THRIFT NOTICE

Each night, empty your pocket or purse of pennies and drop them into an old fish tank or unused umbrella stand.

Ask your bank for a supply of paper tubes designed to hold a roll of 50 pennies each. Deposit these rolls in a savings account from time to time.

Within a few months, you'll realize that this accumulation of odd coins won't amount to anything for years.

RECIPE

Flagging appetite? Try this. Over a hot (not flaming) charcoal fire, broil a thick slab of prime sirloin of beef for three and a half minutes. Dice and place in dog's dish. If he still won't eat, take him to a vet.

New forms for short humor are welcomed by the markets. This is one field in which the writer can experiment with impunity. As an editor, I searched eagerly for original presentations; and as a writer, I twist and torture my mind, constantly seeking fresh ways to express an amusing notion. Incidentally, if you're aiming at the top markets, don't ever end a piece like this: "Why are you looking so funny, dear? Put down that crowbar! I . . . Glmmmmmmpf!" This will almost certainly put the kiss of rejection on it.

Lastly, a piece of humor, no matter how short, should be worked over carefully and thoroughly. Its brevity does not condone haste or carelessness. Restrain that impulse to send everything off at once to a publisher. Write and rewrite, polish and repolish; then put your brain child away for a few days. When you read it again with a fresh eye, is it still warm, still funny? If it isn't, and it won't respond to further rewriting, throw it away. Short humor is about the most expendable of literary properties; and while pride of authorship is commendable, a feeling that every composition is too precious to cast aside is a great handicap in the creative process.

The late Joseph Wood Krutch, former Professor of Dramatic Literature at Columbia University, said: "Anyone who undertakes to write about how one should write is sticking his neck out."

There's mine.

11

CONTESTING

by SELMA GLASSER

For a stamp and a few well-chosen words, you can win trips to Europe, Jamaica, Nassau, Puerto Rico and all over the country. Or how would you like complete gas heat installation in your home, a car, a mink, color TV's, dates with Sid Caesar and Engelbert Humperdinck—and cash (large and small amounts)? All this has happened to me since I've been pursuing the fascinating pastime of contesting!

Word for word, creative writing contests are probably the most lucrative field of writing today. Imagine earning $100 for a limerick, or, better yet, $100 for a last line added to the sponsor's given four lines. Consider the person who recently won an expense-paid trip around the world for three weeks, simply by writing 25 words about a famous liquor. Or the family who jetted to Denmark with

Reprinted courtesy *Writer's Digest* © 1976.

$1,000 spending money for writing the best last line to a jingle. How about the clever housewife sporting a $7,500 mink for writing 50 words on why she's a good girl?

You need not be a top-notch writer or a mental giant to win. Contest opportunities abound, and by being resourceful and selective, you can increase your winnings—and income. With a little time and energy, you can compose that last line, statement or rhyme, and win. And once you win, you'll be hooked for life!

The first prize I won was a vacation at a mountain resort. It was the first time in my life that I had entered a contest. The topic: why I preferred a trip to the mountains. I wrote:

> The seashore with its sand and sea
> Is not the place for me to be,
> My permanent comes out, you see
> And I'm unhappy as can be.
> Where can you find a lake or tree
> A male, perhaps, for company
> But at the mountains, you'll agree!

Naturally, I never quit the hobby after that!

You'll need the usual tools of the literary trade—a good dictionary, a rhyming dictionary and a thesaurus. But most important, you must keep writing. Practical experience is by far the most important asset.

By applying myself diligently, I discovered that timely, topical entries make a hit with the contest judges. Way back in the days of Willie Mays, a detergent manufacturer gave the top prize for a last line that—surprisingly enough mentioned Mays, not the detergent. The winner—"It leaves more time for Willie Mays"—got a brand new car.

PUNS AND PARODIES

Puns and all kinds of word play are the stock-in-trade of the contest entrant, but the stock should be kept not only as fresh as possible but appropriate to the sponsor's product. Contestants were asked to write about Royal Cola. In my prize-winning entry, I fitted my pun to the product, in this way:

I get more energy from this soft drink because it offers more Royal *Colawatts* per glassful.

When a contest required the naming of a sad-looking puppy (and the Mona Lisa was on loan here from the Louvre), I used timely, topical punning in naming the dog "Moana Leasha" and took top prize. Note that this entry combined timeliness with word play.

Kool-Aid asked for a statement about their drink. I began mine, "Kool-Aid's Fountain of Uses . . . ," and walked off with their two-hundred-dollar prize.

Parodies and take-offs on popular expressions are also sure-fire winners. A shampoo contest winner wrote, for $1,000: "The old gray hair ain't what it used to be." A TV set winner wrote about a detergent, "Soapstitutes were clothes-careless." A $300 washer winner wrote: "It banishes summer grimewaves."

A car wax company received these phrases: "Wax is driving me glazy . . . It's the great wipe away . . . It offers wise and shine . . . such glowings on." A ballpoint pen contest inspired these puns: "It doesn't leakaboo . . . proves its point . . . Its heart's in the write space."

The winner of a vacation in Spain recently wrote about a rubbing alcohol: "Shakespeare cried, 'Ay, there's the rub.' and Ann answered, 'It hath-a-way, Willie.' "

STATEMENTS, SLOGANS AND CAPTIONS

When Stella D'Oro asked contestants to state in twenty-five words or less why their cookies were like a trip to the continent, I wrote: "Because they both take dough." My payoff was first prize of a trip for two to Italy and France, which comes to considerably more than $50 a word.

Occasionally, it has been my practice to compose a rhyme when a statement of 25 words or less is required in a typical commercial contest. It creates an interesting variation on the expected prose form. The judges and/or sponsors may then be pleasantly surprised and consider a rhymed entry as an extra form of originality of presentation.

In another Stella D'Oro entry, I used verse in the statement I submitted, and won with the following:

> Their "so near and yet so foreign" appeal
> Of continental "favors" reveal:
> Topflight flavors of European nations
> In sizes and shapes that are STELLA(R) creations!

I'm sure that the parody beginning and the pun on the sponsor's name in the last line helped make this rhymed statement a winner.

When Protein 21 shampoo was introduced, a cash contest was announced for the best twenty-five word statement. The lead line was "How I Beat the Frizzies." Here again I used rhyme to win a prize:

With Protein 21 care,
I've sheen-clean, Wash 'N' Wear hair!

(Note also the use of internal rhyme.)

Here's a winning slogan for multiple sclerosis: "Let your dollars be the key/ To unlock MS mystery!" A winning automobile slogan was: "The real low-down/ slow down!"

When a friend showed me a copy of *Signature,* I spotted a monthly caption contest. The picture showed a dais with two politicians seated in front of a mike. One seemed to be looking away as the other spoke. My cash prize was won by putting these words into the speaker's mouth: "Who are you? You've been seated next to me at the last six press conferences."

Another winner of mine pictured Rockefeller addressing the President and these are the words I had Rockefeller say:

"Just think, centuries from now Charlton Heston will make us famous."

But you don't have to be a punster or rhymer to win. Some sponsors prefer straight statements, and award prizes to simple sentences stacked with sales points. For example, a New Hampshire trip winner wrote why she'd like to own a home in the Granite State: "This traditionally independent progressive state offers natural beauty, cultural facilities, and recreational opportunities with four climate season for leisurely summer sun or invigorating winter fun." A car winner wrote: "I like the new Datsun because it is excitingly redesigned for 'years-to-come' smoothness, comfort and convenience; economical to run, service and repair; Datsun has smooth oriental beauty, with solid occidental practicality."

A short-cut to contest success is *analogy*—that is, the use of terms from an entirely different field or context. For example, one winner used baseball terminology in a cigar contest: "I like El Ropos because with *major league* quality at *minor league* price, they *score* heavily in taste, blend and fragrance—every puff *a home run* in smoking pleasure." There are hundreds of other fields from which likely words and phrases may be selected.

(A helpful source book is *Analogy Anthology,* which contains 65 groups of specialized terms from academic analogus to zodiac analogs, in alphabetic order, for convenient reference and utilization.)

Some time ago, a company selling concentrated orange juice mix offered cash and merchandise for two additional rhymed lines (couplet) to follow the first two, which they gave:

(Company's lines)
    In summer when you're hot and dry,
    Refresh with orange juice—here's why:

I entered this contest and had two winners:

(1) This "concentrated champ"—profuse
     Will yield "live wires" needed "juice!"
(2) In *flaming* heat, its *matchless flavor*
     Gives *burning* pep with *cooling* savor!

By coincidence, both of my winning sets of lines use *analogy.* In the first couplet, *wires* and *juices* are electrical terms; in the second, *flaming, matchless, burning,* and *cooling* normally apply to oven phraseology. This type of verbal device, used sparingly and effectively, often produces prize-winning lines, phrases, sentences, verses, or fillers.

LIMERICKS

A limerick is a five-line verse in which the first, second and fifth lines have three feet and rhyme, and the third and fourth lines have two feet and rhyme. Despite the competition, there is an insatiable and continuing demand for top-notch limericks, as well as for prize-worthy last lines to complete the first four often given in contests for "best last lines." A national magazine once advertised a limerick contest sponsored by Spam, which was cleverly called a SPAMerick Contest. Contestants were required to "dish up" a complete limerick. Here is the way the sponsor announced my first-prize-winning entry in the magazine some months later:

> Herewith is the winner in *Ingenue,*
> Who wrote winning lines in Contest 2
> Rhymes chockful of meat
> (To our ears quite sweet)
> Hormel's happy to pass it on to you!

(The meter of the sponsor's limerick was a little off, but we'll excuse him because he presented the prizes!) Here is my winner:

> Cleopatra with feminine guile
> Said to Tony, "Let's barge down the Nile!"
> Then she packed up some SPAM,
> Bags of popcorn and jam
> To beguile down the Nile in high style!

Have you noticed the very simple triple rhyme in the

last line, the tribute to the sponsor's product, and the casual breeziness of the entire limerick?

The National Safety Council annually publishes a calendar containing unfinished limericks. They award prizes of $100, $50, $25, and thirty $5 prizes every month, from February to December, on a specified safety theme. From my own observation and experience as a winner, I would recommend that submitted lines contain a good follow-through and also some definite safety statement (in rhyme, of course!).

Here is a recent, typical National Safety Council limerick (first four lines) and the three top-prize-winning last lines:

> Pop was showing his kids he could still
> Ride a bike with no hands—well, until
> The front wheel hit a hole
> And he lost all control

$100 line: *With Pro-how not Crow-how show your skill!*
$50 line: *Brag-man's bluff is "kid-stuff" far from skill.*
$25 line: *Wrong to trust skills that "rust"—better drill.*

Observe the techniques of inner rhyme and also note that each winning line could stand independent of the limerick and teach an excellent safety rule by itself. That is perhaps the biggest secret I've discovered by repeated wins in this continuing limerick last-line contest.

Needless to say, some of the techniques overlap, as is exemplified by this prize-winning jingle, with rhyme, analogy, a pun and a sales point: "If harmony is what you crave/ Go get a TUBA Burma-Shave."

Now don't you think this hobby's fun?

It's lucrative for every*won*!

12

PREPARING AND SELLING
YOUR MANUSCRIPT

by A. S. BURACK

Although writing fillers and short humor does not require specialized knowledge or experience, there are some basic techniques for preparing and marketing manuscripts which you will find helpful. The *content* of the material is the editor's chief concern when deciding whether or not to buy a manuscript, but good *form* and neat appearance are always plus factors in editorial eyes. You can also increase your sales by learning as much as possible about markets, by being resourceful in collecting material and by being business-like in submitting manuscripts.

KNOWING THE MARKETS

Every good salesman must know what his customers want to buy. If you hope to sell short items regularly, you should be aware of what the editors are currently purchasing. New writers in the filler and short item field often discover that they are already familiar with many of the existing markets. Your daily or Sunday newspaper or favorite magazine very likely will welcome your submissions. If you or someone in your family reads a trade paper or business magazine, you'll discover that such specialized publications may also be buying short items.

The quickest and easiest way to find out who will buy fillers, humor, light verse, etc., is to study the available market lists. The market section which follows is a comprehensive listing of publications that will buy such items. Other market lists are printed from time to time in journals for writers.

You should also keep checking the publications themselves, since editorial requirements for fillers and short humor change frequently. A magazine may solicit contributions for a particular column for several months—and then stop purchasing, either because the editor has enough items on hand or because the column is to be replaced by a different feature with different needs. Often, requirements for a column may vary from week to week or month to month. *Reader's Digest* sometimes adds new departments, *Redbook, Good Housekeeping* and other magazines from time to time announce special columns which buy short items.

Most of the publications you'll want to study may be found at your local library or newsstand. Libraries subscribe to many different publications, and although current issues generally cannot be taken out, you can keep up with your potential markets by making an occasional visit to the periodical section. Many newsstand dealers understandably object to strangers leafing through dozens of magazines on display, but they are usually willing to let regular customers do some browsing—so patronize one stand as often as you can. Buy something once in a while to retain the dealer's good will. If a magazine is not available at your library or newsstand, you can purchase a sample copy directly from the publisher.

Some writers of short items try to know the needs of many *different* magazines so that they will be able to select a market quickly when they have a suitable idea. Others concentrate on three or four publications they feel they can sell to, and study these carefully. Most writers try to find at least one or two new markets each month—for a change of pace, to replace discontinued markets, or simply to expand their sales possibilities.

COLLECTING MATERIAL

One of the first steps a new writer of short items should take is to set up some method of collecting ideas and information. Perhaps you will decide that a notebook will serve your purpose at the beginning, or possibly you may want a more elaborate filing system.

Some writers keep a file of large envelopes or folders. They decide upon several categories that interest them— either something as specialized as "Bright Sayings of Children" and "Recipes," or more general classifications like "Women's Magazines" and "Outdoor Projects." They then tuck into the files all related material: ideas, information, possible markets, etc. Many writers make a practice of carrying small notebooks with them so that they can jot down an idea the moment they think of one. Later they transfer the notebook pages to the proper files.

You may find it helpful to save printed material that

may later be useful—tags on garments, manufacturers' information sheets, etc. Government pamphlets contain many useful facts; you may request specific pamphlets from the Superintendent of Documents, Government Printing Office, Washington, D. C. 20401, and you may also ask to be put on the free mailing list to receive information about government publications.

HOW TO SUBMIT SHORT ITEMS

In general, the procedure for submitting a short item is the same as that for submitting any manuscript: Prepare a neat, legible manuscript (typed manuscripts are always preferred). Your name and address should be typed in the upper left-hand corner of the first page; the number of words in the upper right-hand corner of the first page. It is not necessary to give the exact number of words in a manuscript. Simply count the number of words in the average line and multiply this by the number of lines on the page. Thus, if you have ten words in an average line, and ten lines of typing, your item is about one hundred words long. The title of the manuscript should be centered, and your by-line goes beneath the title. Often the only title you will have is the title of the column to which you are submitting the item—"Life in These United States," "Quotable Quotes," etc. The top of the first page of your manuscript will look like this:

John J. Jones   80 words
54 Willow Road
Anytown, New York 10028
              A New Way to Store Scrap Lumber
                       by John J. Jones

Often, writers of short items will have more than one item to submit at a time. Each item should be typed double-spaced on a separate sheet, with your name and address on each sheet. If the items are on separate sheets, editors are able to pass around several items for consideration by different departments. Also, if an editor wishes to buy just one item out of the group submitted, he doesn't have to hold a page with other material on it.

How many short items should be submitted at one time? Some writers decide this by discovering how many they can mail for a single first-class stamp. Remember that you must include a return envelope when weighing your material. In general, not more than four to six items should be submitted together. Many editors dislike reading large batches of material from one person and may feel that an over-prolific writer does not spend enough time on each item.

Short items do not have to be submitted on full sheets of paper. You may divide an 8½ x 11 sheet in half, but do not try to crowd an item onto too small a piece of paper. Leave margins of at least one inch on all sides. Minor corrections may be made in ink, but in general, it is always better to retype a short item than to submit a soiled or much-corrected manuscript. Editors are always grateful for the manuscript that is neat and easy to read.

Along with your manuscript, enclose a self-addressed, stamped envelope large enough to contain your manuscript, and bearing sufficient postage so that the editor can return your manuscript to you if he cannot use it. Address your item to a department, column or specific editor. You don't need to know the name of the editor; "Filler Editor" or "Handyman Editor" will do.

When you are mailing an item for a particular column in a magazine, be sure to check the rules for submission in a recent issue of the magazine. Sometimes a publication has special requirements; others may ask for artwork to accompany written materials. *Mechanix Illustrated,* for example, wants some tips illustrated by rough drawings; crafts magazines often ask for diagrams for crafts projects.

You do not need to send a letter to accompany your manuscript. Editors understand that you are submitting an item for their consideration when it is addressed and sent to them. Nor do you have to indicate that you are enclosing a self-addressed, stamped envelope for the return of your material if they cannot use it—editors know what the envelope is for. *Never* tell the editor that you hope he buys an item because you need money, etc., or indicate that he ought to accept an item because your friends read his magazine and think your item is perfect for it. Such letters stamp you as a rank amateur and editors are not favorably influenced by them.

However, it is a good idea to enclose a covering letter if you have a unique background or training that makes you especially qualified to write on a particular subject. For instance, if you are a professional dietician and submit special recipes, let the editor know about your background and training so that he is aware that you speak with authority on your subject.

Do not send a manuscript to more than one market at a time. If a manuscript is returned by the first market you select, then you may submit it to a second, etc. Many magazines do not return short items at all, and indicate this policy somewhere on their pages along with a statement noting the amount of time that must elapse before an item can be considered rejected. You must observe this waiting period before you submit your item to another market.

Make a carbon copy of any item you submit. (It is especially important to retain carbon copies of items sent to publications that do not return manuscripts.) In cases where magazines require printed clippings, record the pertinent facts about these on a file card. (If a magazine follows a no-return policy, it generally makes no exception, even if you hopefully enclose a self-addressed stamped envelope—so you may forfeit those printed clippings.)

Keep track of the date when you mail a manuscript so that if a publication states, "Items not accepted within six weeks can be considered rejected," you know when your six-week waiting period will expire. For income tax purposes, you'll want to know how much money you've received and who paid you. If a holiday or seasonal item doesn't sell one year, you may want to know where you submitted it and what the editor's comments were. Sometimes an editor will indicate that he is currently overstocked, and request that you resubmit at a later date.

Perhaps the simplest method of keeping a record is to use the back of your carbon copy of the manuscript. Note the name and address of the magazine and the date the item was submitted. If the item is accepted, note this and the amount received. If the item is rejected, note this, plus any pertinent editorial comment. Clip any related papers—letters, sales contracts, etc.—to the carbon copy. When an item is accepted, you will probably want to transfer the carbon from a "Submitted" file to an "Accepted" file, so plan to keep at least two files.

Another method often used by writers calls for two files

of 3 x 5 cards. The cards in one file contain the history of each item submitted (the title, number of words, where and when submitted, etc.). When an item is accepted, the appropriate information is noted on its card, which is then transferred to the other file.

Most editors try to accept or reject manuscripts as promptly as possible, but often you will have to wait as long as six weeks for a report. Occasionally even more time will go by without any word from an editor. If you are sure that a magazine makes it a policy to return manuscripts, and you haven't received any report in two months, write a polite note to the editor, asking if he received your submission. Enclose a self-addressed stamped envelope for his reply. Sometimes manuscripts do get lost in the mail and often reports are delayed because of staff absences or changes in editors; if you do inquire about a manuscript, most editors will try to let you know promptly what has happened.

Sometimes, when a magazine accepts your item, you will receive a contract or release that you must sign and return. The contract usually asks you to certify that the item is original, and states the terms of the sale. You are safe in accepting the terms of a contract from any reputable publisher.

IT IS TIME TO BEGIN

You alone can supply the essential qualities that will insure your success in writing and selling fillers and short humor. You must be willing to keep writing and sending out your manuscripts. Don't allow yourself to become discouraged—many an item has been sold on its fifteenth or even twentieth trip to market. Look and listen for ideas, write them up, pick appropriate markets, and then submit your manuscripts. Only then can you feel the sense of accomplishment and anticipation that all writers share. Your manuscript may come back with a rejection slip— send it to the next market on your list! But you may also receive a check—not only a reward in itself, but a promise that your name and writing will appear in print. From that moment on, you are a selling writer.

Part II
Where to Sell

NOTE

The following list gives markets for a wide variety of short material: fillers, short humor, short inspirational pieces, jokes, cartoons, light verse, children's material (puzzles, crafts, etc.), contests, and other brief items. The listings give information on what types of short items each publication buys, length requirements, and rate and time of payment. Only publications which *pay* for short items have been listed.

Although extreme care has been taken to give accurate information, the needs of editors vary from time to time, and there will undoubtedly be some changes in the requirements as listed. Some new magazines may come into existence, and others now being published may be suspended. A few well-known magazines are currently not purchasing short items, and they asked not to be listed at this time, but their needs may change. From time to time many of the high-circulation publications announce special departments using fillers and short humor, and some magazines run contests periodically. Writers should watch their pages for these items. For all publications it is usually advisable for writers to check recent issues before submitting manuscripts.

MANUSCRIPT MARKETS

AIR PROGRESS—7950 Deering Ave., Canoga Park, CA 91304.
Cartoons for private pilots. Pays $25, after publication.

ALASKA, MAGAZINE OF LIFE ON THE LAST FRONTIER—Box 4-EEE,
Anchorage, AK 99509.
Short features, with photos, on Alaska by residents. Pays $10 to $50, on
publication.

ALIVE!—Christian Board of Publications, P.O. Box 179, St. Louis, MO 63166.
Cartoons, puzzles, brainteasers, word games, short poetry. Pays $6 for
cartoons, to $8 for puzzles and fillers, 25¢ a line for poetry.

AMATEUR ARCHAEOLOGIST—P.O. Box 8012, Wichita, KS 67208.
Cartoons to interest amateur archaeologists. Pays $25. Enclose stamped
return envelope.

THE AMERICAN FIELD—222 West Adams St., Chicago, IL 60606.
Short fact items and anecdotes on outdoor sports and field trials for bird
dogs. Pays varying rates, on acceptance.

AMERICAN FRUIT GROWER—37841 Euclid Ave., Willoughby, OH 44094.
Personal-experience pieces, 200 to 500 words, on commercial production
and selling of fruit. Pays varying rates.

AMERICAN JOURNAL OF NURSING—10 Columbus Circle, New York, NY
10019.
Short verse, humor, epigrams, and jokes for "Time Off" column. Pays $5
to $10 per item.

AMERICAN LEGION MAGAZINE—1608 K St. N.W., Washington, DC 20006.
Address Parting Shots Editor.
Anecdotes, to 300 words; humorous light verse, to 16 lines, epigrams. Pays
$20 for anecdotes, $2.50 a line for verse, $10 for epigrams.

AMERICAN VEGETABLE GROWER—37841 Euclid Ave., Willoughby, OH
44094.
Personal-experience pieces, 200 to 500 words, on commercial production
and selling of vegetables. Pays varying rates.

THE AMERICAN WEST—20380 Town Center Ln., Cupertino, CA 95014.
Ed Holm, Editor.
Illustrated articles, 1,000 words, on unusual people, places or events of Old
West, for "Collector's Choice." Pays $76.

ARIZONA—120 East Van Buren St., Phoenix, AZ 85004.
Sunday magazine of *The Arizona Republic*. Short fillers, humor, cartoons,
related to Arizona. Pays before publication.

ARIZONA'S HOST—7302 East Sixth Ave., Scottsdale, AZ 85251.
  Fillers, short humor, 150 to 200 words, on Arizona and the Southwest.
  Pays various rates.

ARMY MAGAZINE—1529 18th St., N.W., Washington, DC 20036. L. James
    Binder, Editor-in-Chief.
  Essays, humor, news reports, first-person anecdotes, on military subjects.
  Pays from 7¢ a word, $5 to $25 for anecdotes, on publication.

THE ATLANTIC—8 Arlington St., Boston, MA 02116.
  Sophisticated humorous or satirical pieces, 1,000 to 3,000 words. Some
  light poetry. Pays varying rates, on acceptance.

BABY CARE—52 Vanderbilt Ave., New York, NY 10017. E. Podsiadlo,
    Editor.
  Short items for "Focus on You" (500 words), "Family Corner" (100
  words). Short poetry, cartoons. Pays $10 to $25.

BABY TALK—66 East 34th St., New York, NY 10016.
  Short features on child care.

THE BAWL STREET JOURNAL—10 Hanover Sq., New York, NY 10005.
  Annual paper (published in June) that parodies Wall Street, its brokers
  and their firms. Uses humorous, often sarcastic articles, to 300 words, on
  investing, business and finance. Considers material between February and
  April 30.

THE BEAVER—Hudson's Bay House, Winnipeg, Manit., Canada R3C 2R1.
    Helen Burgess, Editor.
  Fillers, 700 to 1,000 words, on historical or modern aspects of northwest
  Canada and Arctic regions. Pays on acceptance.

BICYCLING!—P.O. Box 4450, San Rafael, CA 94903.
  For cycling enthusiasts. Humor, photos. Pays $1 per column inch, extra for
  photos, on publication.

BITS AND PIECES—Box 746, Newcastle, WY 82701. Mabel E. Brown, Editor.
  Fillers, 500 to 1,000 words, on history of Wyoming and surrounding states.
  Source must be given. Pays in copies.

BOYS' LIFE—North Brunswick, NJ 08902.
  How-to features, to 750 words, with photos, on hobbies, crafts, science,
  outdoor skills, etc. Pays from $150.

BREEZY—See *Humorama, Inc.*

BUCKS COUNTY PANORAMA—57 West Court St., Doylestown, PA 18901.
  Humor and cartoons on Delaware Valley area. Pays various rates.

CALIFORNIA HIGHWAY PATROLMAN—1225 8th St., Suite 150, Sacramento, CA 95814.
Cartoons. Pays $10, on publication.

CAPPER'S WEEKLY—616 Jefferson St., Topeka, KS 66607.
Short, 500 to 700-word human interest and personal experience articles; letters on women's interests, for "Heart of the Home," jokes, cartoons. Pays on publication.

CARTOON PARADE—See *Humorama, Inc.*

CATHOLIC DIGEST—P.O. Box 3090, St. Paul, MN 55165.
For "Hearts Are Trumps," original accounts, under 300 words, of true cases where unseeking kindness was rewarded. For "Open Door," true incidents by which persons were brought into the Church. For "The Perfect Assist," original reports of tactful remarks or actions. For "People Are Like That," true accounts illustrating goodness of human nature. Pays $50 per item. Amusing tales of parish life for "In Our Parish." Pays $20 per item. Pays $4 for "Flights of Fancy," picturesque figures of speech, and for "Signs of the Times," amusing signs. Give exact source. Regular jokes and fillers, average payment $10. All payment on publication. Submissions not acknowledged or returned.

CATS—P.O. Box 4106, Pittsburgh, PA 15202.
Poems, to 30 lines, preferably light, about cats. Pays 30¢ a line, on acceptance.

CB DIGEST—676 North La Salle St., Chicago, IL 60610.
CB (citizens band radio) cartoons and jokes. Pays varying rates, on acceptance and on publication.

THE CB TIMES—1005 Murfreesboro Rd., Nashville, TN 37217.
Fillers, jokes, short humor about citizens' band radio. Pays on acceptance.

CHANGING TIMES: THE KIPLINGER MAGAZINE—1729 H St. N.W., Washington, DC 20006.
Original, unpublished humorous epigrams, topical quips, one or two sentences, for "Notes on These Changing Times." Pays $10 per item.

CHATELAINE—481 University Ave., Toronto, Ont., Canada M5N 1V5.
Light verse. Pays $10 to $25, on acceptance.

CHARLOTTE MAGAZINE—P.O. Box 15843, Charlotte, NC 28210.
Fillers to 750 words relevant to North Carolina. Pays on publication.

CHILD LIFE—1100 Waterway Blvd., Box 567B, Indianapolis, IN 46206.
Verse, puzzles, games, mazes, tricks, for 7- to 11-year-olds. Pays around 3¢ a word, on publication.

CHILDREN'S PLAYMATE—1100 Waterway Blvd., P.O. Box 567B, Indianapolis, IN 46206.
Verse, puzzles, games, mazes, tricks, for 3- to 8-year-olds. Pays around 3¢ a word, on publication.

CHORAL PRAISE—See *The Church Musician.*

THE CHRISTIAN ADVENTURER—Messenger Publishing House, P.O. Box 850, Joplin, MO 64801.
Inspirational fillers, to 300 words, and Bible puzzles, for teen-agers. Pays ½¢ a word, on publication.

CHRISTIAN HERALD—40 Overlook Dr., Chappaqua, NY 10514.
Personal-experience pieces, 500 words; unusual anecdotes; poetry, 4 to 24 lines; photos with an inspirational message. Pays $5 to $15.

THE CHRISTIAN HOME—201 Eighth Ave. South, Nashville, TN 37202.
United Methodist. Articles, 800 to 1,000 words, relating to family living. Seasonal, inspirational or humorous verse, to 16 lines. Pays $10 to $15, 50¢ a line for poetry, on acceptance.

CHRISTIAN LIFE—Gundersen Dr. and Schmale Rd., Wheaton, IL 60187.
News items, 100 to 200 words, on trends, ideas, personalities and events of interest to Christians. Photos. Pays on publication.

THE CHURCH MUSICIAN—127 Ninth Ave. North, Nashville, TN 37234. W.M. Anderson, Editor.
For Southern Baptist music leaders. Fillers. Pays around 2¢ a word, on acceptance. Same address and requirements for *Gospel Choir* and *Choral Praise* (for adults), and *Opus One* and *Opus Two* (for teen-agers).

CLASSIC—551 Fifth Ave., New York, NY 10017.
Magazine about horses for sport and pleasure. Short items for "Comment" column. Pays $25, on acceptance.

COLUMBIA—Box 1670, New Haven, CT 06507.
Journal of the Knights of Columbus. Humor and satire, to 1,000 words; captionless cartoons. Pays to $100, $25 for cartoons, on acceptance.

COLUMBIA JOURNALISM REVIEW—700 Journalism Bldg., Columbia University, New York, NY 10027.
Amusing mistakes in news stories, headlines, etc. (original clipping required), for "Lower Case." Fillers, 250 words, on non-New York media happenings, for "National Notes." Pays $10 to $25, on acceptance.

THE COUNTRY GENTLEMAN—1100 Waterway Blvd., Indianapolis, IN 46202.
Appropriate fillers relating to rural living, crafts, environment, gardening, etc. Pays on publication.

COUNTRY WORLD—Box 1770, Tulsa, OK 74102.
Sunday supplement of the *Sunday World*. Farm, suburban, homemaking pieces, to 800 words, with photos. Pays from $10 per column, on publication. Query.

CREEM—P.O. Box P-1064, Birmingham, MI 48012. Robert Duncan, Acquisitions Editor.
Off-beat news items, to 500 words; cartoons. Pays varying rates.

CRICKET—P.O. Box 100, LaSalle, IL 61301.
For children 6 to 12. Uses puzzles, riddles, crafts, recipes, humorous verse and limericks. Pays up to 25¢ a word, on publication.

CRUISING WORLD—Box 452, Newport, RI 02840.
Fillers, poetry, cartoons, photos and photo-essays related to technical and recreational aspects of cruising under sail. Pays on publication.

CRUSADER—1548 Poplar Ave., Memphis, TN 38104.
Southern Baptist. For boys 6 to 11. Hobbies, games, nature pieces. Pays 2½¢ a word, on acceptance.

CYCLE WORLD—1499 Monrovia Ave., P.O. Box 1757, Newport Beach, CA 92663.
Humor, 1,500 to 2,000 words, of interest to motorcycle enthusiasts. Racing reports, 400 to 600 words, with photos. Cartoons; news items on motorcycle industry, legislation, trends. Pays $75 to $100 per printed page, on publication.

DAILY MEDITATION—Box 2710, San Antonio, TX 78299. Ruth S. Paterson, Editor.
Inspirational, nonsectarian fillers, to 350 words. Pays from ½¢ a word, on acceptance.

DAIRY HERD MANAGEMENT—P.O. Box 67, Minneapolis, MN 55440.
Fillers. Pays from $10.

DELL CROSSWORD PUZZLES—245 East 47th St., New York, NY 10017. Kathleen Rafferty, Editor.
Mysteries, 500 words, with clues for solution. Pays $25, on acceptance.

DENTAL MANAGEMENT—757 Third Ave., New York, NY 10017.
Time- and money-saving tips for dental assistants, for "Ask Juli—Time-saving Tips." Pays $5.

DIXIE-ROTO—*The Times-Picayune,* New Orleans, LA 70140.
Humorous shorts involving children from Louisiana or Mississippi, for "Bright Talk." Documented historical anecdotes related to the South. Pays $20 for anecdotes, $2 to $3 for shorts.

DOWN EAST—Camden, ME 04843.
True anecdotes and stories about Maine, to 300 words, for "It Happened Down East." Pays $10. Recollections of Maine incidents, to 300 words, with black-and-white photo, for "I Remember," $10. "Room With a View," 1,000 words, pays $35. Amusing or informative observations of contemporary Maine, which lend themselves to editorial comment, for "North by East" section. Payment is determined by length and is on acceptance.

EBONY—820 South Michigan Ave., Chicago, IL 60605.
For "Speaking of People," items to 200 words, on blacks in jobs heretofore closed to blacks. Material must describe job, how obtained, training, etc. Human-interest angle helpful. Pays $20.

ELITE—1280 St. Marc St., Suite 308, Montreal, Que., Canada H3H 2G1.
Men's magazine. Fillers, newsbreaks, and ironic or offbeat items. Pays on publication.

THE ELKS MAGAZINE—425 West Diversey Pkwy., Chicago, IL 60614. Jeffrey Ball, Editor.
General-interest humor, 1,500 to 2,500 words, for a family audience. Non-political satire. Pays from 10¢ a word.

THE EMPIRE MAGAZINE—*Denver Post,* Denver, CO 80201.
Fillers, with photos, of interest to Rocky Mountain readers. Pays 4¢ to 5¢ a word, $10 per photo.

EXPECTING—52 Vanderbilt Ave., New York, NY 10017. E. Podsiadlo, Editor.
Anecdotes about pregnancy, for "Happenings." Sophisticated light verse. Pays $10, $5 to $10 for verse.

FAMILY CIRCLE—488 Madison Ave., New York, NY 10022. Patricia Curtis,
Copy Director.
Humor, how-to and inspirational pieces, to 1,500 words.

FAMILY DIGEST PARISH MONTHLY (formerly *Family Digest*)—Noll Plaza,
Huntington, IN 46750. Robert A. Willems, Editor.
Catholic. Humorous anecdotes. Pays $5, on acceptance.

THE FAMILY FOOD GARDEN—Route 1, Box 877, McCourtney Rd., Grass
Valley, CA 95945. George S. Wells, Editor.
Fillers and cartoons on home food gardening; some recipes. Pays modest
rates, on acceptance.

THE FAMILY HANDYMAN—1999 Shepard Rd., St. Paul, MN 55116.
Tips and shortcuts, 100 to 300 words on do-it-yourself projects. Pays $5
to $15, on publication.

FARM JOURNAL—Washington Sq., Philadelphia, PA 19105.
Verse, 4 to 8 lines. Humor. Subjects should deal with the farm or the farm
family. Pays on acceptance.

FAST SERVICE—757 Third Ave., New York, NY 10017.
Fillers, photos on fast-food restaurants. Pays various rates.

FATE—Clark Publishing Co., 50 Hyacinth Pl., Highland Park, IL 60035.
Factual fillers, to 200 words, on strange or psychic happenings. True
stories, to 300 words, on psychic or mystic personal experiences. Pays $1
to $10.

FIELD AND STREAM—383 Madison Ave., New York, NY 10017.
Features, to 2,500 words, on hunting, camping and fishing. How-to pieces,
to 1,000 words. Pays from $500 for features, $250 for how-to pieces.

FLING—1485 Bayshore Blvd., Suite 400, San Francisco, CA 94124.
Men's magazine. Humor and satire, 1,500 to 3,000 words. Pays from $100.

"40" MAGAZINE—120 Sylvan Ave., Englewood Cliffs, NJ 07632.
Short essays, 100 to 300 words, for "Quick Takes," interesting news or
reviews to interest persons in government, business etc. Pays on publication.

FUN HOUSE—See *Humorama, Inc.*

GALLERY—99 Park Ave., New York, NY 10016.
Men's magazine. Short humor, satire. Pays from $350, after acceptance.
Query.

GARCIA FISHING ANNUAL—329 Alfred Ave., Teaneck, NJ 07666. Robert E. Stankus, Editor.
Humorous pieces on fishing. Pays on acceptance.

GASOLINE NEWS—100 North Grant St., Columbus, OH 43215.
Clippings on service stations, car wash and snowmobile industries. Pays 50¢ per clipping, on publication. Query.

GAZE—See *Humorama, Inc.*

GIRLTALK—See *Talk.*

GOLF DIGEST—495 Westport Ave., Norwalk, CT 06856.
Short fact items, anecdotes, quips, jokes, light verse related to golf. True humorous or odd incidents, to 200 words. Pays from $15, on acceptance.

GOLF MAGAZINE—380 Madison Ave., New York, NY 10017.
Fillers, to 750 words, and short humor, on golf. Cartoons. Pays from $25, on acceptance.

GOOD HOUSEKEEPING—959 Eighth Ave., New York, NY 10019. Robert M. Liles, Features Editor.
Pays $5 and up for light verse. Very short humorous prose items for humor page and back of book fillers. Pays from $10 to $100.

GOSPEL CARRIER—Messenger Publishing House, P.O. Box 850, Joplin, MO 64801.
Inspirational fillers, to 300 words. Pays ½¢ a word, on publication.

GOSPEL CHOIR—See *The Church Musician.*

GOURMET MAGAZINE—777 Third Ave., New York, NY 10017.
Sophisticated light verse with a food or drink angle. Pays on acceptance.

THE GREEN PAGES—641 West Fairbanks, Winter Park, FL 32789. Blanche Dormandy, Editor.
Humor, jokes, and fillers related to rehabilitation of the handicapped. Pays on publication.

GRIT—Williamsport, PA 17701.
Short articles, 300 to 800 words, with photos, on small towns, personal courage, free enterprise, patriotic subjects, unusual occupations or hobbies. Pays 5¢ a word, extra for photos, on acceptance.

GUIDEPOSTS—747 Third Ave., New York, NY 10017. Dina Donohue, Senior Editor.
Anecdotal fillers, to 250 words, with spiritual or inspirational point. Pays $10 to $25.

HANDBALL—4101 Dempster St., Skokie, IL 60076.
Fillers, 30 to 40 words, on handball and handball players. Cartoons, photos. Pays from $25, on acceptance.

HOCKEY ILLUSTRATED—333 Johnson Ave., Brooklyn, NY 11206. Jim McNally, Editor.
Fillers, puzzles, short humor. Pays on publication.

HOME LIFE—127 Ninth Ave. North, Nashville, TN 37234. George Knight, Editor.
Southern Baptist. Personal-experience pieces, 100 to 500 words, on family relationships. Pays 2½¢ a word, on acceptance.

HOSPITAL PHYSICIAN—488 Madison Ave., New York, NY 10022.
Short items by physicians, for "Here's How I Do It," "What's Wrong with This Patient?," "Your Next Step?," and "Pediatricks." Pays $10 to $15.

HOW TO, THE HOMEOWNER'S HANDBOOK—P.O. Box 4015, Stamford, CT 06907. Jim Liston, Editor.
Captioned photos, illustrating worksaving, or problem-solving device, for "Problem Solvers." Pays $25.

HUMORAMA, INC.—100 North Village Ave., Rockville Centre, NY 11570.
Topical satire, epigrams, humorous fillers, to 600 words. Light verse, to 24 lines. Pays $1.50 for one-line fillers, 60¢ a line for verse, 5¢ a word for prose, before publication. Same address and requirements for *Joker, Pop Cartoons, Pop Jokes, Cartoon Parade, Laugh Riot, Quips, Stare, Gaze, Fun House, Zip, Cartoon Fun & Comedy, Wink,* and *Breezy.*

HUNTING—Petersen Publishing Co., 8490 Sunset Blvd., Los Angeles, CA 90069.
How-to fillers on hunting. Pays $50.

THE ILLUSTRATOR—Sunday School Dept., MSN #176, 5 NW, 127 Ninth Ave. North, Nashville, TN 37234.
Fillers, photos, on archaeology, geography and history of biblical lands. Pays 2½¢ a word, on acceptance.

ISAAC ASIMOV'S SCIENCE FICTION MAGAZINE—Box 13116, Philadelphia, PA 19101. George Scithers, Editor.
One page fillers, from short shorts to limericks, appropriate for science fiction magazine. Pays on acceptance.

JACK AND JILL—1100 Waterway Blvd., P.O. Box 567B, Indianapolis, IN 46206. William Wagner, Editor.
Poems, short plays, puzzles, games, science and craft projects, for 5- to 12-year olds. Instructions for activities should be clearly written, accompanied by diagrams and a list of materials needed. Pays varying rates, on publication.

THE JEWELERS' CIRCULAR-KEYSTONE—Clifton Way, Radnor, PA 19089.
Features, 200 to 300 words, on a single activity that built sales or cut costs for a jeweler. Pays $10, on acceptance.

JOKER—See *Humorama, Inc.*

LADY'S CIRCLE—21 West 26th St., New York, NY 10010.
Fillers, 600 words, with black and white photos, on antiques, bringing up children, gardening, nostalgia, etc. "Sound Off" department pays $10. "Readers' Exchange Cookbook" pays $5.

LAUGH RIOT—See *Humorama, Inc.*

LEARNING—530 University Ave., Palo Alto, CA 94301. Address Swap Shop Editor.
Items, to 600 words, on original teaching ideas. Pays $25.

THE LOOKOUT—8121 Hamilton Ave., Cincinnati, OH 45231. Mark A. Taylor, Editor.
Inspirational or humorous shorts, 100 to 500 words, Pays 3¢ a word.

LOUISVILLE TODAY—125 North Adams St., Louisville, KY 40204.
Fillers, 150 words, short humor, cartoons. Pays after acceptance.

McCALL'S—230 Park Ave., New York, NY 10017.
Fillers on ideas for better living, for "Survival in the Suburbs." Pays $50. Manuscripts are not acknowledged or returned. Phone number must be included with submissions. Occasionally buys light verse.

MAGAZINE OF THE MIDLANDS—*Omaha World Herald,* World-Herald Sq., Omaha, NE 68102.
Regional-interest humor, from 300 words. Pays on publication.

MAKE IT WITH LEATHER—Box 1386, Fort Worth, TX 76101.
How-to fillers on leathercraft, for "Tips and Hints." Pays $10.

MARRIAGE AND FAMILY LIVING—St. Meinrad, IN 47577.
Anecdotes, to 150 words, on husband-wife or parent-child relationships. Short jokes. Pays $5, on publication. Manuscripts are not returned or acknowledged.

MATURE YEARS—Methodist Publishing House, 201 Eighth Ave. South, Nashville, TN 37202.
Poems, cartoons, puzzles, jokes, anecdotes, to 300 words, for older adults. Pays 3¢ per word, on acceptance.

MECHANIX ILLUSTRATED—1515 Broadway, New York, NY 10036.
Single photos with captions and tips for shortcuts in shop, garage or home, for "It's New" and "Home & Shop Shorts." Cartoons for "Freddie Fumbles." Ideas for inventions, for "Inventions Wanted." Fillers, to 500 words. Pays $5 to $75.

MODERN BRIDE—One Park Ave., New York, NY 10017.
Humorous pieces, 500 to 1,500 words, and poetry, for brides. Pays on acceptance.

MODERN MATURITY—215 Long Beach Blvd., Long Beach, CA 90802. Hubert C. Pryor, Editor.
Money-saving ideas and how-to and crafts tips, for "Tips Worth Considering." Quizzes, cryptograms, riddles, brainteasers, etc., for "Fun Fare." Quotes from people over 54. Seasonal material (submit 6 months in advance). Pays $5 to $20.

MODERN PHOTOGRAPHY—130 East 59th St., New York, NY 10022.
How-to pieces, 200 to 300 words, with photos, on photography. Pays $25 to $50, on acceptance.

MPLS.—512 Nicollet Mall Bldg., Suite 615, Minneapolis, MN 55402. William Kienzle, Editor.
Short humor, puzzles, photo-essays on Minneapolis region. Pays various rates.

NATIONAL ENQUIRER—Lantana, FL 33462. Address Fillers Editor.
Short humorous fillers, quotations (give source), witticisms, anecdotes, tart comments. Pays $15. Occasional contests.

NATIONAL GUARDSMAN—One Massachusetts Ave. N.W., Washington, DC 20001.
True Army and Air Force anecdotes, for "Tales from the Troops." Pays $10, on publication.

NATIONAL LAMPOON—635 Madison Ave., New York, NY 10022.
Short humor; satire.

NATIONAL REVIEW—150 East 35th St., New York, NY 10016.
Satire, to 900 words. Pays $35 to $75, on publication.

NATIONAL SAFETY COUNCIL—444 North Michigan Ave., Chicago, IL
60611.
Monthly cash prizes totaling $325 awarded from February to December for
last lines to limericks printed in their calendars, which may be obtained
from them for $1.

THE NATIONAL STAR—See *The Star.*

NEBRASKALAND—2200 North 33rd St., Lincoln, NE 68503. Lowell
Johnson, Editor.
Verse of interest to Nebraska residents. Cartoons on outdoor subjects. Pays
$5 for cartoons. No payment for verse.

THE NEW YORKER—25 West 43rd St., New York, NY 10036.
Amusing mistakes in newspapers, books, magazines, etc. Entertaining anecdotes. Pays from $5, extra for headings and tag lines, on acceptance.

NORDEN NEWS—Norden Laboratories, 601 West Cornhusker Hwy., Lincoln,
NE 68521. Patricia Pike, Editor.
Jokes, photos related to veterinary medicine. Pays on publication.

NRTA JOURNAL—215 Long Beach Blvd., Long Beach, CA 90801. Hubert C.
Pryor, Editor.
Short verse, humor, "Find-the-Word" puzzles, tips, crafts, cartoons, for
older readers. Pays $5 to $50.

THE OHIO MOTORIST—P.O. Box 6150, Cleveland, OH 44101.
Humorous poems, 4 to 6 lines, on motoring and vacation topics. Pays $7 to
$10.

ON THE LINE—616 Walnut Ave., Scottdale, PA 15683.
Light verse, 8 to 24 lines, cartoons, puzzles, quizzes, human-interest photos
with captions, for 10- to 14-year-olds. Pays $4 to $8 for verse, from $4 for
puzzles and quizzes, $7.50 to $15 for photos.

OPERA NEWS—The Metropolitan Opera Guild, 1865 Broadway, New York, NY 10023. Robert Jacobson, Editor.
Humorous anecdotes on all aspects of opera. Pays on publication.

OPUS ONE—See *The Church Musician.*

OPUS TWO—See *The Church Musician.*

ORBEN'S CURRENT COMEDY—801 Wilmington Trust Bldg., Wilmington, DE 19801. Send manuscripts to Robert Orben, 2510 Virginia Ave. N.W., Apt. 701-N, Washington, DC 20037.
Original, funny, performable one-liners and brief jokes on news, fads, topical subjects, etc. Pays $3. Stamped, self-addressed envelope required for return of manuscript.

ORGANIC GARDENING AND FARMING—33 East Minor St., Emmaus, PA 18049.
Fillers, 100 to 500 words, on gardening experiences: how-to's, solution of problems, etc. Material for various departments; news items. Pays $25 to $50, before publication.

OUI—919 North Michigan Ave., Chicago, IL 60611.
Men's magazine. Short pieces for "Openers." Pays various rates.

OUR FAMILY—BOX 249, Dept. E. Battleford, Sask., Canada SOM 0E0.
Catholic. Humor, verse. Pays 3¢ a word, on acceptance.

OUTDOOR LIFE—380 Madison Ave., New York, NY 10017.
Short instructive or informative items on hunting, fishing, camping gear, boats, outdoor equipment. Photos. Pays on acceptance.

PARENTS' MAGAZINE—52 Vanderbilt Ave., New York, NY 10017.
Humorous children's sayings, for "Out of the Mouths of Babes." Short items on solutions of child care-related problems (allowances, nap-taking, etc.), for "Family Clinic." Pays $5 to $10, on publication.

PENTHOUSE—909 Third Ave., New York, NY 10022.
Adult magazine. Sexy humor, to 5,000 words. Pays from 20¢ a word, on acceptance.

PLAYBOY—919 North Michigan Ave., Chicago, IL 60611. Address Party Jokes Editor or After Hours Editor.
Jokes. Also short, humorous items and typos. Include printed source. Pays $50, in publication, for "After Hours" items.

PLAYERS—8060 Melrose Ave., Los Angeles, CA 90046. Joe Nazel, Editor.
For black men. Humor, satire. Movie, theater and record reviews, 100 to 500 words. Pays on publication.

PLAYGIRL—1801 Century Park East, Suite 2300, Century City, Los Angeles, CA 90067.
Fillers, 500 to 800 words, humor, satire and cartoons, for contemporary women.

POP JOKES—See *Humorama, Inc.*

POPULAR PHOTOGRAPHY—One Park Ave., New York, NY 10016.
Illustrated how-to pieces, for "Photo Tips." Pays $25, on publication.

POPULAR SCIENCE MONTHLY—380 Madison Ave., New York, NY 10017.
Short fact items and hints, with photos or sketches, for "Taking Care of Your Car" and "Short Cuts and Tips." Pays $25, on acceptance.

POWER FOR LIVING—1825 College Ave., Wheaton, IL 60187.
Comments on contemporary issues, 300 to 500 words, for "Viewpoint" column, personal-experience articles reflecting a Christian interpretation of life. Pays from $50. Query.

PROCEEDINGS—U.S. Naval Institute, Annapolis, MD 21402. Clayton R. Barrow, Jr., Editor.
Short humorous anecdotes for members of Navy. Pays $25, on acceptance.

PRO-TEEN—Light and Life Press, Winona Lake, IN 46590.
For young teens. Fillers, some poetry. Pays on acceptance.

PUBLICIST—Public Relations Aids, Inc., 221 Park Ave. South, New York, NY 10003. Lee Levitt, Editor.
Short case histories of successful national public-relations campaigns and projects, 400 to 800 words; cartoons; fillers; photos; humor relating to professional public relations. Pays after publication. Queries preferred.

QUIPS—See *Humorama, Inc.*

QUOTE MAGAZINE—P.O. Box 4073, Station B., Anderson, SC 29621.
Light verse, to 4 lines, of value to ministers, toastmasters, club leaders and other public speakers.

RAINBOW—American Baptist Board of Education and Publication, Valley Forge, PA 19481.
For 8- to 11-year-olds. Poetry, puzzles, prayers, cartoons, art. Pays to 3¢ a word, on acceptance.

READER'S DIGEST—Pleasantville, NY 10570.
True and previously unpublished anecdotes for "Life in These United States," "Humor in Uniform," "Campus Comedy" and "All in a Day's Work." Pays $300. Also buys contributions for "Toward More Picturesque Speech," "Laughter, the Best Medicine," "Quotable Quotes," "Personal Glimpses." Payment for original material is $15 per *Digest* two-column line, with a minimum of $35, on publication. Contributors should watch magazine for announcements of other departments. Address submissions to the Editor of each department. No fillers can be acknowledged or returned.

REFLECTION—Box 788, Wheaton, IL 60187.
Publication of Pioneer Girls. Cartoons, quizzes, games, photos, with Christian emphasis. Pays various rates, on acceptance.

THE RETIRED OFFICER—1625 Eye St. N.W., Washington, DC 20006.
For military retirees. Uses humor, from 1,000 words. Pays from $25, on publication. Query.

ROAD KING—P.O. Box 319, Park Forest, IL 60466.
Jokes and cartoons, for "Loads of Laughs"; recipes, for "Wives Are Winners." Pays $5 for jokes, $25 for cartoons, $10 for recipes.

ROLL CALL—428 Eighth St. S.E., Washington, DC 20003.
Humorous items on Congress; anecdotes, puzzles, quips on political subjects. Pays on acceptance.

ROTARIAN—1600 Ridge Ave., Evanston, IL 60201. Willmon L. White, Editor.
"Stripped Gears" uses fillers and light verse. Humorous articles, 1,200 words, for business and professional men. Pays top rates. Query.

RUNNER'S WORLD—P.O. Box 366, Mountain View, CA 94040. Joe Henderson, Editor.
For middle- and long-distance competition or fitness runners. Short opinion pieces for "Runner's Forum." Pays on publication. Query.

ST. JOSEPH MESSENGER—P.O. Box 288, Jersey City, NJ 07303.
Humorous fillers, 90 to 100 words, and verse, 4 to 40 lines. Pays 1¢ a word, on acceptance.

SAN FRANCISCO—120 Green St., San Francisco, CA 94111.
Fillers, 250 to 500 words, on Bay Area and northern California. Cartoons. Pays $25 to $50, on publication.

THE SATURDAY EVENING POST—1100 Waterway Blvd., Indianapolis, IN
46202. Frederic A. Birmingham, Managing Editor.
Humor and satire, 1,500 to 2,000 words; cartoons, light verse for "Post
Scripts," short quizzes (boxed and illustrated), two-paragraph anecdotes.
Pays varying rates.

SCOPE—Augsburg Publishing House, 426 South 5th St., Minneapolis, MN
55415.
Journal of the American Lutheran Church Women. Religious, humorous,
or inspirational fillers. Pays on acceptance.

SEA—1499 Monrovia Ave., Newport Beach, CA 92663.
Humor on boat operation and cruising destinations in western states. Pays
10¢ a word, on acceptance. Query.

SEVENTEEN—850 Third Ave., New York, NY 10022.
Fillers, to 500 words, for "Mini-Mag." Articles, 800 words, by teens, for
"In My Opinion." Fact and fiction, 20 to 200 words, by teens, for "Free
For All." Photos, cartoons, poetry, by teens. Pays varying rates, on accep-
tance.

SKEPTIC—812 Presidio Ave., Santa Barbara, CA 93101.
Essays, reports and documented opinion, to 1,000 words, for "Short Stuff."
Payment negotiable.

SKIING MAGAZINE—One Park Ave., New York, NY 10016.
Articles, 500 to 1,000 words, on skiing of the past; personal anecdotes,
humorous vignettes. One-paragraph fillers on skiing oddities. Articles,
1,200 to 1,500 words, on skiing experiences in distant places, for "Letters
From." Pays from 10¢ a word, on acceptance.

SMALL WORLD—Volkswagen of America, 818 Sylvan Ave., Englewood
Cliffs, NJ 07632.
Anecdotes, to 100 words, about Volkswagen owners' experiences; car-
toons, humorous photos of Volkswagens. Pays from $15, on acceptance.

SNOTRACK—534 North Broadway, Milwaukee, WI 53202. Bill Vint, Editor.
Magazine of United States Snowmobile Association. Short humor and cartoons. Pays $15 to $25 for cartoons, varying rates for humor.

SOAP OPERA DIGEST—420 Lexington Ave., New York, NY 10017. Ruth J.
Gordon, Executive Editor.
Crossword puzzles ("Soapuzzles") and recipes with a soap-opera tie-in.
Pays various rates. Query.

SPORTS AFIELD—250 West 55th St., New York, NY 10019.
Unusual, useful tips, 100 to 700 words, with photos, on hunting, fishing,
camping, boating, etc. Pays $50 to $400, on acceptance.

THE STAR (formerly *The National Star*)—730 Third Ave., New York, NY 10017.
Unusual news stories, with photos, for broad family readership. Pays varying rates.

STARE—See *Humorama, Inc.*

SUNDAY DIGEST—850 North Grove Ave., Elgin, IL 60120. Darlene McRoberts, Editor.
Humorous or inspirational Christian anecdotes, to 500 words. Timely vignettes (submit seasonal material 12 months in advance) and quotations, to 300 words. Short poems, jokes and epigrams, on Christian virtues or frailties. Pays $2 to $25, on acceptance. Stamped, self-addressed envelope required for return of manuscript.

SUPER NEWS!—1515 Broadway, New York, NY 10036.
Fillers for "The Greatest Compliment," "Reader's Home Hints," "Make the Most of It!" (recycled household furnishings), "My Favorite Pepper-Upper," "How to Say I Love You," "Super-Fast Supper," "Penny-Saver Recipes." Pays $20. Manuscripts not returned.

SURFER MAGAZINE—Box 1028, Dana Point, CA 92629.
News items, to 50 words, with photos, on surfing. Humorous poems, cartoons. Pays 4¢ to 10¢ a word, on publication.

TALK (formerly *Girl Talk*)—380 Madison Ave., New York, NY 10017.
Fillers, short, humorous verse, cartoons, for women. Pays 8¢ a word.

TENNIS—495 Westport Ave., Norwalk, CT 06856.
Fillers, humor. Pays from $25, on publication. Query.

TENNIS ILLUSTRATED—4222 Campus Dr., Newport Beach, CA 92660.
Fillers, verse, humorous articles on tennis personalities, etc. Pays 10¢ a word, on publication. Query.

TENNIS USA—Chilton Co., Chilton Way, Radnor, PA 19089. Robert L. Gillen, Editor.
Cartoons, jokes, puzzles and fillers, on tennis. Pays to $25, on acceptance.

TODAY'S CHRISTIAN PARENT—8121 Hamilton Ave., Cincinnati, OH 45231. Wilma L. Shaffer, Editor.
Creative children's activities; short items on Christian living, for "Happenings at Our House." Quips, short poems. Pays varying rates, on acceptance.

TRAILER BOATS—1440 West Walnut, Compton, CA 90220. Ralph Poole, Editor and Publisher.
Fillers, humor and jokes, on boats. Pays 7¢ to 10¢ a word, on publication.

THE TRAVEL ADVISOR—387 Park Ave. South, Suite 8, New York, NY 10016.
   Filler-length travel tips providing inside travel information on costs, accommodations, etc. Pays $15 to $25.

TRUE CONFESSIONS—205 East 42nd St., New York, NY 10017.
   Fillers, 300 to 800 words, of interest to young wives, for "Feminine Side of Things." Pays from $50, on acceptance.

TRUE ROMANCE—205 East 42nd St., New York, NY 10017. Barbara J. Brett, Editor.
   Articles, 300 to 700 words, of interest to young blue-collar women. Pays flat rate.

TRUE STORY—205 East 42nd St., New York, NY 10017.
   Short humorous or inspirational personal-experience pieces, for "Women Are Wonderful." Features on home and children; light verse. Pays 5¢ a word.

TRUE TREASURE—P.O. Drawer L, Conroe, TX 77301.
   Fillers, 100 to 250 words, on lost mines and buried or sunken treasure, for "Treasure Nuggets." Pays $12.50.

TV GUIDE—Radnor, PA 19088.
   Short humor, one magazine page in length, on television, for "TV Jibe." Pays varying rates.

UNITY MAGAZINE—Unity School of Christianity, Lee's Summit, MO 64063.
   Fillers, to 500 words. Pays on acceptance.

VIVA—909 Third Ave., New York, NY 10022. Jill Goldstein, Executive Editor.
   Humor, to interest modern women. Pays from $250. Query.

WEIGHT WATCHERS MAGAZINE—635 Madison Ave., New York, NY 10022.
   How-to pieces, quizzes and cartoons, on weight loss. Pays on acceptance.

WESTART—Box 1396, Auburn, CA 95603.
   Features and current news items, 350 to 500 words, on crafts and fine arts. No hobbies. Pays 30¢ per column inch, on publication.

WESTERN RESERVE MAGAZINE—Box 243, Garrettsville, OH 44231. Mary Folger, Editor.
   Fillers on little-known Western Reserve history. Pays on publication.

WINK—See *Humorama, Inc.*

WOMAN'S DAY—1515 Broadway, New York, NY 10036.
Short items on instructive family experiences, for "Neighbors"; practical suggestions for homemakers. Photos. Pays $25.

WOMEN'S CIRCLE HOME COOKING—Box 338, Chester, MA 01011. Barbara Hall Pedersen, Editor.
Magazine for cooks. Humorous fiction, to 400 words; hints; anecdotes; fillers; verse to 8 lines. For "Cooks' Photo Album," recipe with snapshot of cook. Pays on publication.

THE WORKBASKET—4521 Pennsylvania, Kansas City, MO 64111.
Illustrated how-to articles, 200 to 400 words, on crafts. Brief instructions for crafts women can make and sell (include selling price), for "Women Who Make Cents." Pays 4¢ a word for how-to pieces, $5 for instructions, on acceptance.

WOW—American Baptist Board of Educational Ministries, Valley Forge, PA 19481.
For 6- to 7-year-olds. Poetry, puzzles, cartoons, Bible verses. Pays on acceptance.

YACHTING MAGAZINE—50 West 44th St., New York, NY 10036. William W. Robinson, Editor.
Short fillers and anecdotes. Pays modest rates, on publication.

YANKEE MAGAZINE—Dublin, NH 03444.
Features, to 400 words, on small New England businesses and hobbies. Unusual or humorous stories, 500 to 2,500 words, with photos, related to New England. Pays $15 for short features, $25 to $400 for articles, $15 to $25 per photo.

YOUNG ATHLETE—Box 513, Edmonds, WA 98020. Dan Zadra, Editor.
Dedicated to boys' and girls' amateur sports. Jokes for "Sports Humor." Brief profiles of boys and girls who have achieved sports success. Pays on publication.

YOUNG JUDEAN—817 Broadway, New York, NY 10003. Barbara Gingold, Editor.
For 8- to 12-year-olds. Fillers, humor, reviews relating to Jewish-American life, Jewish history, Israel, etc. Pays various rates.

YOUNG MISS—52 Vanderbilt Ave., New York, NY 10017.
How-to pieces, to 100 words, particularly on things to make with odds and ends, for teen-age girls. Pays $5, on acceptance.

ZIP—See *Humorama, Inc.*

DATE DUE

FEB 2 8 1980			
JAN 2 1 1982			